"Jentezen Franklin reveals ⸺ and discerning men and women c⸺ ⸺ves of those around them. Allow *Right People, Right Place, Right Plan* to alter your perspective and speak to your heart."

—*Joyce Meyer*
Best-selling author and Bible teacher

"Jentezen Franklin, in this exciting and life-changing book, reveals how men and women of discernment forever change the lives of people in their circles of influence. If you read one book this year, make it *Right People, Right Place, Right Plan.*"

—*John Hagee*
Best-selling author
Senior Pastor, Cornerstone Church, San Antonio, Texas

"As a leader, there are few topics more difficult to navigate than that of discernment. And trying to teach others about it is even more harrowing. But in his book, *Right People, Right Place, Right Plan*, Jentezen Franklin has unveiled the key that unlocks this perplexing subject. Whether you are a leader in the church, business world, education, or home, this book will give you the real-life knowledge you need to hear the voice of God and make the most of your full potential in every situation you face."

—*Ed Young*
Senior Pastor, Fellowship Church
Author of *Outrageous, Contagious Joy*

RIGHT PEOPLE
RIGHT PLACE

RIGHT PLAN

DISCERNING THE VOICE OF GOD

RIGHT PEOPLE
RIGHT PLACE

RIGHT PLAN

DISCERNING THE VOICE OF GOD

JENTEZEN
FRANKLIN

WHITAKER HOUSE

RIGHT PEOPLE, RIGHT PLACE, RIGHT PLAN:
Discerning the Voice of God
new trade paperback edition

Jentezen Franklin Ministries / Kingdom Connection
P.O. Box 315
Gainesville, GA 30504
www.jentezenfranklin.org

ISBN: 978-1-60374-328-0
Printed in the United States of America
© 2007 by Jentezen Franklin

Whitaker House
1030 Hunt Valley Circle
New Kensington, PA 15068
www.whitakerhouse.com

The Library of Congress has cataloged the hardcover edition as follows:

Franklin, Jentezen, 1962–
  Right people, right place, right plan : discerning the voice of God / Jentezen Franklin.
    p. cm.
  Summary: "Helps believers develop spiritual discernment in order to make wise life-decisions in accordance with the will of God in areas such as marriage, career, finances, and family"—Provided by publisher.
  ISBN 978-0-88368-276-0 (trade hardcover : alk. paper) 1. Discernment (Christian theology) 2. Decision making—Religious aspects—Christianity. I. Title.
  BV4509.5.F746 2007
  248.4—dc22
                                      2007009214

2 3 4 5 6 7 8 9 10 11 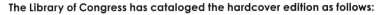 18 17 16 15 14 13 12 11

DEDICATION

This book is dedicated to the six darlings in my life:
my wife, Cherise, without whom I would be nothing;
my four daughters, Courteney, Caressa,
Caroline, and Connar;
and my son, Drake.

May the lessons in this book be a part of the spiritual legacy
I leave behind for all of you.

APPRECIATIONS

A special thanks to three of the greatest men of God I have ever been privileged to know: Tommy Tenney, T.F. Tenney, and Steve Munsey. Their mentorship in my life has been profound.

To my congregation at Free Chapel, which has loved, supported, and believed in me for almost two decades, I want to express my sincerest gratitude.

Lastly, a special thanks to my television partners, who enable me to take the gospel around the globe.

CONTENTS

Part I

THE GIFT OF DISCERNMENT

Chapter One

Your Internal Compass

Man shall not live by bread alone;
but man lives by every word that proceeds
from the mouth of the LORD.
—Deuteronomy 8:3

In the middle of China, an ordinary person repeatedly drops a small shard of iron onto a leaf and watches as the leaf floats on the water. Inexplicably, the leaf spins around until it points in the same direction every time. Historians and archaeologists now believe that this is how the compass, the original navigational tool, was discovered—years before the Bible was ever written.

They had no concept of north and south—the alignment naturally sought by the metallic shard—and for millennia no one would discover why this solitary piece of metal behaved as it did. Yet, years later, the compass would be embraced by sailors and travelers needing the precise direction to lead them to their ultimate destination. Before the compass, these wanderers could only look around and set their course by the physical markings around them. They had no idea that there was an internal force—in this case, the earth's magnetic field—that influenced that small piece of iron.

Inside every believer, ordinary and extraordinary, there is a compass—an internal force—placed by God, waiting to be discovered and used for His glory. When you learn to utilize and trust this valuable resource, you will find that you can better navigate the stormy seas and cloudy skies of life.

Whom should I marry?

What will I do with my life?

Do I take this job?

Should I invest my money in this opportunity?

Life, it seems, is a never-ending cycle of decisions that can alter the entire direction of our destinies. How freeing it would be if we had access to an internal compass that would fix the direction of our lives to true north. Without it, we are left to look around and set our course by the markings of our physical world—our emotions and hunches, and the voices of those who would want to influence our journey.

What if we could learn to rely on the compass set in place by our Creator? What if we could discern the voice of God in our lives? God desires to speak into your life, if only you would learn to recognize His voice. By the power of His Holy Spirit, He has given you all you need to set a course for your life that will lead you to the right people, the right places, and the right plan in order to achieve His perfect will for your life.

THE VOICE OF GOD

In Genesis, God said, "Let there be," and there was! The heavens, the earth, the land, and the seas were all spoken into existence by the voice of God. Then we read: *"God said, 'Let Us make man in Our image, according to Our likeness'"* (Genesis 1:26). Thus, man was made in the image of God, who then put

14

His life within man. *"And the L*ORD *God formed man of the dust of the ground, and breathed into his nostrils the breath of life; and man became a living being"* (Genesis 2:7). As the image of God, man was different from the rest of creation, for he was a self-determining being. Man had a voice in how his life would turn out. He was created in the likeness of God.

Man demonstrated this immediately as he began to name the animals. Just like his Creator, man could also talk and call things by a name. Man was not a god himself, but he could speak like God, and Godlike force was in his voice because God had *"breathed into his nostrils the breath of life."* God breathed His voice into Adam.

But Adam and Eve were not alone in the garden. Satan slithered in and immediately went to work driving a wedge to separate man and woman from the voice of God. Notice his approach: *"Now the serpent was more cunning than any beast of the field which the L*ORD *God had made. And he said to the woman, 'Has God indeed said?'"* (Genesis 3:1). Satan knew that if he was going to defeat the human race, he had to separate man from the voice of God. You know the rest of the story. Satan said, *"In the day you eat of it your eyes will be opened, and you will be like God"* (Genesis 3:5). Does anything strike you as strange there? How about the fact that they were already like God! They had been created in the likeness of God.

Here we get a sneak peek into the strategy of the enemy in your life: he will do whatever he can to get you to listen to his voice instead of the voice of God. He would like nothing better than to suggest the direction of your life. He will tell you that you have to be someone else—someone other than who God wants you to be. Why else would he suggest to Eve that she could *"be like God,"* implying that Eve was not already made in the likeness of God? Perhaps that is why so many people spend their whole lives trying to impress others by being something that they are not. Their lives are racked with frustration and regret. They don't understand that God made them in His image. You don't have to be somebody you are not—you are already what He wants.

After the fall, God came walking through the garden in the cool of the day. What did Adam and Eve do? They hid from the voice of God. From that moment on, the Old Testament becomes a chronicle of mankind's love/hate relationship with the voice of God.

> You don't have to be somebody you are not—you are already what He wants.

In Exodus, God spoke with Moses through a burning bush and, later, dictated the Ten Commandments complete with flashes of lightning and smoke. Scripture says the people trembled and told Moses, *"You speak with us, and we will hear; but let not God speak with us, lest we die"* (Exodus 20:19). Look at how well Satan's plan was working. Man went from speaking with God in the garden to being afraid of His voice. Satan had so perverted man's relationship with God that they thought the very sound of His voice would kill them. Today, Satan's plan is no different. He will convince you that if you listen to God it will kill your relationships, your career, and your fun. He will tell you that the Word of God will take life from you.

Eventually, things got so bad that God said, in effect, "Okay, you don't want to hear My voice anymore? You don't want Me to speak to you? Fine. I'm done." With that, His Word stopped. Scripture ceased—bringing an abrupt end to the Old Testament.

And for four hundred years, the voice of God went silent.

Eventually, that silence was broken by *"the voice of one crying in the wilderness"* (Matthew 3:3). The book of John leaves no doubt that God was ready to speak again: *"In the beginning was the Word, and the Word was with God, and the Word was God.... And the Word became flesh and dwelt among us"* (John 1:1, 14). God had broken the silence, and now His voice had skin and bones.

When Jesus started His ministry by being baptized in the Jordan River, it was God's voice that confirmed Jesus as His Son: *"And suddenly a voice came from heaven, saying, 'This is My beloved Son, in whom I am well pleased'"* (Matthew 3:17).

Can't you just imagine the demons trembling? The voice that was in the garden, the voice that walked *"in the cool of the day"* (Genesis 3:8), that voice was back on the planet speaking into the lives of His beloved creation. The Word of God was back to display its power. Jesus spoke to a storm and it stopped. Jesus spoke to Lazarus and he walked out of a grave. Jesus spoke to a fig tree and it withered. When His followers expressed amazement at the demise of the tree, Jesus informed them, *"Assuredly, I say to you, if you have faith and do not doubt, you will not only do what was done to the fig tree, but also if you say to this mountain, 'Be removed and be cast into the sea,' it will be done"* (Matthew 21:21).

It was official. Not only was God's voice active again, but it was also free to work within and through the lives of those who called upon Him. God was not finished working through the lives of His people. In fact, He was just getting started.

GOD'S VOICE IN YOUR LIFE

How can you discover that special, internal direction that

God uniquely gave to you? What is God's plan for your life? Many women today can feel anything but special as they try to fulfill the ever-present demands of career, church, and family. They feel left out, stressed out, and frazzled. Most men today are confused as the world tries to feminize them, and then expects them to be "real men" by satisfying their every desire. They feel marginalized, emasculated, and under attack.

God sees you as extraordinary, and He desires to use you in extraordinary ways. He is searching for men and women who dare to believe they can make a difference. Today, the body of Christ (the church) must open up their spiritual ears to hear and recognize the voice of the Almighty. Could it be that God wants to use you as a key player in His kingdom in these last days?

I was six years old, taking a bath with my G.I. Joe action figures one Saturday night, when I began to sing Bill Gaither's song, "The King Is Coming." My mother, who was listening, entered the bathroom and said, "Jentezen, our church musicians are out of town tomorrow and your dad asked me to take care of the music. I have everything lined up but the special music for the offering. Will you sing that song tomorrow for the offertory?" She kept on pushing me, not taking no for an answer.

"I will if you pay me twenty dollars," I finally said.

"It's a deal!"

My mother read between the lines, sensing something about her son's destiny through her spiritual discernment. Yet, neither one of us knew that singing that song the next day would launch me into my ministry.

Believe it or not, I still remember that day. Tears were flowing as the congregation was moved. The tender touch of God came upon my life. Later I began to sing in the choir and play the drums, the sax, and the piano, which led to my accepting the call to preach.

Today, I pastor an amazing church filled with thousands of people, and I reach millions by television. But it was all triggered by the amazing discernment of my mother.

There are things that you know that you can't explain. First John 2:20 says, *"But you have an anointing from the Holy One, and all of you know the truth"* (NIV). All believers have an anointing, a spiritual touch of God, that provides them with remarkable insight. Through the Holy Spirit,

> **All believers have an anointing from God that provides them with insight.**

from whom flows all the gifts, graces, and superior knowledge of God, you have inside information on what God's will is.

God has given every ordinary believer an extraordinary gift. He has given you an internal compass to guide and discern things about your children, your spouse, your family, your career, and your finances.

This discernment is not from human wisdom; it is from God. In the next few chapters, you will learn how to:

- activate the voice of the Holy Spirit.

- trust your inner voice of discernment.

- apply discernment in everyday life.

- make a profound difference in your loved ones' lives by just being you.

As you will soon see, this will be the most important life lesson you've ever experienced as you fulfill your assignment in becoming the man or woman God created you to be.

Chapter Two

A FEEL FOR THE REAL: DISCERNING GOD'S VOICE

They should seek the Lord, in the hope that they might grope for Him and find Him, though He is not far from each one of us.

—Acts 17:27

Have you ever been reading a book at home near a light when a little moth flitted by you? You barely noticed it; it's a tiny little insect.

Did you know there is only one time in Scripture where God is compared to a moth? The prophet Hosea pastored God's people during one of the most prosperous eras of Israel. Eventually, in the midst of all their prosperity, Israel began to backslide, and Hosea warned them, *"Therefore I [God] will be to Ephraim like a moth"* (Hosea 5:12). But just two verses later, he says, *"For I [God] will be like a lion to Ephraim"* (verse 14). Hosea's prophecy to Israel reveals a great concept about discernment. It demonstrates how God speaks to His people.

If you will be receptive and obedient to the Holy Spirit's voice when God wants to guide you, He will never hit you with anything more powerful than a moth. However, if you are insensitive and resistant to His voice, He will come to you like a lion. God is so gentle. His first choice in getting your attention is to gently nudge you in the right direction. He doesn't want to have to roar to be heard. If you opened your closet door and a moth flew out, you might not even notice it. But if you were greeted by the roar of a lion, that would probably get your attention.

It's a beautiful thing to be gently led by the Holy Spirit. As feathery as a moth, God is trying to direct you and show you His way; His preference is not to resort to the lion to chase you in the right direction—but He will. *"I will return again to My place till they acknowledge their offense. Then they will seek My face; in their affliction they will earnestly seek Me"* (Hosea 5:15).

When we don't follow the gentle leadings of the Word of God and of the Holy Spirit, we then grow insensitive to His presence. Insensitive people wait for the lion to come before they will believe God is telling them anything. Some people say, "Well, if God doesn't want me to do it, then He needs to send something to stop me." Again, God's desire is to use the gentle leadings of the Holy Spirit (the moth), but if we remain stubborn or insensitive to this, He will get our attention one way or the other (the lion).

A dramatic example of this moth/lion approach is found in 2 Samuel. King David's rebellious son, Absalom, sent for Joab in order to send him with a message to his father. But Joab would not come. Absalom sent for him a second time, but still Joab would not obey. Finally, Absalom sent his servants to set Joab's barley fields on fire. With his fields burning, Joab came running to Absalom and asked, "Why have your servants set my field on fire?" Absalom replied, in effect, "I sent for you once, then sent for you a second time, and still you didn't come. So, I set your barley fields on fire as a last resort to get your attention." (See 2 Samuel 14:29–31.)

A FEEL FOR GOD'S VOICE

By now you are probably wondering, *How do I activate this discernment in my life? How do I recognize the prophetic whispers of God?*

I once heard about a U.S. Treasury officer who had the job of identifying counterfeit dollar bills. He said, "The key to identifying a false bill is to spend hours and hours handling the real thing." In other words, you have to get a "feel for the real" if you want to identify the fake.

As you spend time with God praying and studying His Word, you will develop a feel for the voice of God. You will instantly begin to recognize when something does not feel right in your spirit.

In Genesis 27, Isaac could have avoided being deceived if he had had a "feel for the real." Jacob, Isaac's younger son, wanted the blessing that belonged to his older brother, Esau. In order to get it, Jacob had to convince his father to speak the blessing over him. So, Jacob's mother, Rebekah, came up with a clever scheme to fool the aging Isaac, whose eyesight was beginning to fail. Jacob mimicked Esau's voice and covered his arms with animal pelts in order to disguise himself as his older, and more hairy, brother. By pretending to be Esau, Jacob deceived his father and obtained the blessing that was traditionally reserved for the firstborn child. (See Genesis 27:22.) Slightly suspicious at this strange sounding voice, Isaac felt Jacob's arm to assure himself that this was, in fact, Esau. Notice, the old man could have discerned the fraud if he had trusted his ears. We must be careful because often the voice of error can sound nearly identical to the voice of truth.

You have to learn to trust your spiritual ears. Jesus said, *"The sheep follow him* [the shepherd], *for they know his voice"* (John 10:4). Isaac knew something wasn't right when he heard Jacob's voice. He felt Jacob's arm and was deceived by the hairy texture. But spiritual truth cannot necessarily be judged by outward circumstances. Although Isaac was old enough to recognize deception, we need to realize that we are never too old to be deceived. We will never get to the place where we don't have to fine-tune our spiritual sensitivity. You need to handle the Word of God enough to know truth from error.

> You must learn to trust your spiritual ears. People often mistake other voices for God's.

People often mistake other voices for God's voice. The gift of discernment separates the false voices from the real. Some things just don't feel right. It doesn't necessarily mean God is not speaking to you, but if there is a reservation in your spirit, you should wait for God to give you the green light and confirm your feelings before proceeding.

If you feel that something is not right, it could be that it is not according to God's timing. The prodigal son would have gotten his inheritance without experiencing any sorrow if he had waited on his father's timing. Acts 17:27 says, *"They should seek the Lord, in the hope that they might grope for Him and find Him, though He is not far from each one of us."* Just like the treasury officer, we can become so familiar with the voice of God that we are able to immediately recognize the counterfeit voice of Satan when we hear it.

FALLING FOR THE COUNTERFEIT

Have you ever thought you heard God tell you something, only to find out later that you didn't hear from God at all? Until you learn to accurately discern God's voice, you're bound to have a few mistakes.

Not too long ago, I suffered a humbling experience in this area. My wife and I had gone out for the evening. We had left the kids at home with strict instructions about what was permissible and what was not. As it was Christmastime and a lot of candles were sitting around the house, one of the instructions was not to play with matches. We were very clear: there was to be no lighting of candles.

When we arrived home from our evening out, we were shocked to discover that some of the candles had been burned. We knew this because the guilty party had left a trail of melted wax on the hardwood floors. I quickly called the kids in for a lineup and interrogation.

"Who lit these candles?" I asked.

They all denied it. I explained that if they confessed, their punishment would be less severe. Still, no one admitted it. I then went down the list of names one by one. "Did you do it?" All five children denied any involvement. My wife and I knew one of them was not telling the truth. We asked them repeatedly, but still no confession. We were beginning to get upset, not so much because of the candles, but because we knew one of them was flat-out lying.

The atmosphere grew more intense by the minute. We warned the kids of the dangers of lying, and I preached every sermon I knew on the subject. By the time I got through with my little lecture, I had them all dangling by a thread over the hot flames of hell! Repeatedly, I warned, "This is your last chance. Who did it?"

To our amazement, only silence filled the room. But we weren't done. Our next tactic was to separate the kids, hoping one of them would crack and "rat" on the guilty one.

After talking to each of the kids, it seemed to us that our oldest daughter was skirting the truth. We zeroed in like two hardened, NYPD detectives. We peppered her with one question after another, trying to obtain a confession, or at least to blow her flimsy story out of the water.

Although her story stayed the same, so did the mask of guilt that I perceived on her face. I was convinced she was lying to me. Finally, we got the break in the case we'd been looking for when her sister Caroline entered the room. She said, "Just admit it, Courteney. I didn't see you burning the candle, but I saw you watching TV in that room and touching the candle."

At last, an eyewitness! To our amazement, she still denied it. Finally, being the all-wise father, I pronounced judgment: "Courteney, you don't have to admit it. I feel in my spirit that you did it. I feel like God has revealed to me that you're the one."

I gave her a spanking and sent her to her room. Before she left the room I warned her, "Courteney, you can't fool the Holy Spirit. You can fool your parents, your teachers, and other authority figures, but you can't fool God. He always knows the truth."

Caroline came to us an hour later in tears. She admitted, "I did it. I'm sorry. I didn't want to get in trouble. It was me!"

The entire family gathered to remind me that I had just spanked an innocent child, and even worse, I did it because I felt God was telling me she was guilty.

"I thought you felt it in your spirit, Dad," one of them said. From across the room, another one accused, "Yeah, Dad, God told you to whip the wrong kid, right?"

I apologized to my daughter. I was sorry I had misjudged her, and I told her the discipline would count as a credit for her in the future. I was fairly sure she would need it one day. As for Caroline, let's just say that her conscience felt better, but her bottom didn't. Over the years, this incident has become one of the family jokes that we still laugh about today. But it serves as a reminder that discerning the voice of God may take some trial and error.

THE INNER PERSON

There are so many voices in the world. There are the voice of God, the voice of the devil, the voices of people, and your own inner voice. How do you discern between God's voice and all the others? How do you know the difference between a word from the Lord and too much pizza or, even worse, gas?

The Bible tells us, *"God is not the author of confusion"* (1 Corinthians 14:33). In the Old Testament, it was easy. Whenever God wanted the Israelites to go in a certain direction, He just moved the cloud that guided them. When the cloud moved, they moved. When the cloud stayed, they stayed. (See Numbers 9:21–22.)

It is a little more complex today. The cloud of the Old Testament has moved within. *"The spirit of a man is the lamp of the LORD, searching all the inner depths of his heart"* (Proverbs 20:27). The way God speaks and leads us is through our spirits. We have to be spirit-conscious in order to hear God's voice and receive His direction. First Thessalonians 5:23 says, *"May the God of peace Himself sanctify you completely; and may your whole spirit, soul, and body be preserved blameless at the coming of our Lord Jesus Christ."* We are a spirit, living within a body, and we possess a soul, which is our mind, will, and emotions.

In the Old Testament, God dwelt within a temple with an outer court, an inner court, and a Holy of Holies. But under the new covenant, He has a people for His temple. Our body is the outer court, our soul—or mind—is the inner court, and our spirit is the holy of holies. God now dwells in a three-room house: body, soul, and spirit.

> God leads not by your carnal mind or your flesh, but by your spirit.

When God leads you, He does so not by your carnal mind or by your flesh, but by your spirit. When you are born again, your spirit is born again. Ephesians 3:16 says, *"That He would grant you...to be strengthened with might through His Spirit in the inner man."*

First Peter 3 speaks of the hidden person of your heart: *"Rather let it be the hidden person of the heart, with the incorruptible beauty of a gentle and quiet spirit, which is very precious in the sight of God"* (verse 4). Therefore, you have this hidden, inner person inside of you. It is your eternal spirit. Because your inner spirit is born again, it is more finely "in tune" with God's Spirit than your flesh is. You can't make your inner person enjoy sin. If you start to do something wrong, your inner voice will say, "Hey, what are you doing? I don't like that."

Before you were born again, it never bothered you to do certain things; but now that you are born again, God is residing within your inner man and wants to make you like Jesus. Your spirit connects with God and has a voice, and you need to start listening because your success depends not on being led by your mind, your emotions, or your flesh, but by your spirit.

God has placed some indicators—almost like a spiritual alarm system—within our spirits. Here are five indicators you need to recognize in order to discern God's voice.

1. Your spirit can be stirred.

In Acts we read, *"Now while Paul waited for them at Athens, his spirit was provoked within him when he saw that the city was given over to idols"* (Acts 17:16). Notice it wasn't necessarily Paul who was stirred up and provoked, but his spirit.

Does God ever stir you up about something or somebody? Maybe it's a friend you haven't seen or someone you haven't thought about in a long time, but God begins to stir the person up in your heart. Sometimes, that is God's voice speaking to your spirit, urging you to reconnect with that person because He needs you to minister to him or her. Similarly, He can use these stirrings to show you a place to go, a task to complete, or a calling for your life.

2. You can be led by your spirit.

In Romans it says, *"Those who are led by the Spirit of God are sons of God"* (Romans 8:14). Sometimes, God will give you *leadings* within your spirit. When your spirit is led, the Holy Spirit is urging you to do something. When you are Spirit-conscious, God can use you to do great things, whether it is sharing the gospel with a receptive listener or sending $20 to someone you just feel might need it.

3. Your spirit can have purpose.

Returning to Acts, it says, *"When these things were accomplished, Paul purposed in the Spirit, when he had passed through*

29

Macedonia and Achaia, to go to Jerusalem" (Acts 19:21). Paul purposed, not in his mind or in his flesh but *"in the Spirit."* In John 4:24 it says, *"God is Spirit, and those who worship Him must worship in spirit and truth."* We connect with the Spirit of God directly through our spirit, not through the flesh and not through the soul, or mind. Therefore, if you are going to do what God wants you to do, you must purpose it in your spirit, not in your mind or emotions. If I purpose in my flesh to worship God, then I won't do much worshipping. If I purpose in my flesh to go to church, then I won't go very often. But when I purpose in my spirit to worship God, it gets my unwilling body out of bed and focuses my unruly mind on God once I get to church.

When we started building our new worship facility, I purposed in my spirit that we were going to build it. Usually there is a time of divine misery before there is a divine change. I remember feeling an urgency about the building program. I began to receive scriptural confirmation and a stirring in my spirit that God was saying, "Now is the time to build."

Some people said we could not do it; however, when purpose gets in your spirit, all things are possible. Your spirit is connected to the Spirit of God. You can't let your flesh or your mind tell you what you're going to do. You must purpose in your spirit to obey the voice of God and do what He has called you to do.

4. You can be bound in your spirit.

Acts 20:22 declares, *"And see, now I go bound in the spirit to Jerusalem, not knowing the things that will happen to me there."* Paul's spirit was bound to Jerusalem. He didn't know if he would be welcomed or rejected—it didn't matter. When God wants to put you somewhere, He binds you in your spirit to that place.

30

I'm bound in the spirit to the church that I pastor; I'm bound in the spirit to my wife. When God binds you in the spirit, it is very difficult to leave because your spirit is tied to that place or person. Don't ever let your mind or emotions make you walk away from something to which God binds you in spirit. Stay the course and don't quit. Don't give up, because you might miss out on God's mighty plan.

Don't just go to any church; let God bind you in your spirit to a place. Places matter—God created places before He created people. God specifically created the garden of Eden for Adam and Eve and placed them there. (See Genesis 2:7–8.) Many people have location frustration; they're in the wrong place. Let God bind your spirit to the right place, the right people, and the right plan for your life.

5. Your spirit can give you peace about the right direction.

Second Corinthians 2:12–13 says, *"Furthermore, when I came to Troas to preach Christ's gospel, and a door was opened to me by the Lord, I had no rest in my spirit."* Just because a door is wide open doesn't mean you're supposed to walk through it. This is where you need the Holy Spirit's guidance. Do you realize that if Paul had continued to go in the direction he was going, toward Asia, he might never have gone to Macedonia and to Rome? Thus, Europe, the United States, and the Western world would not have received the gospel when they did and may have even remained pagan.

The door was wide open, but Paul said, *"I had no rest in my spirit."* Sometimes, determining God's will is this simple: if you don't have rest in your spirit, don't do it. A lack of divine rest in your spirit is usually God's way of saying no.

If you don't have rest in your spirit about a relationship or a major decision that you're about to make, then I encourage you to give yourself some time to pray. *"Whoever believes will not act hastily"* (Isaiah 28:16). I have learned that God is always right. If I follow His urging, He never misleads me. Remember, God has promised to give wisdom to His children if they will seek it. (See James 1:5.) His desire is that you would hear His voice.

Chapter Three

THE NOD OF GOD:
DISCERNING GOD'S WILL

In all your ways acknowledge Him,
and He shall direct your paths.

—Proverbs 3:6

I s this God's will or not?

This is a question you will have to confront on more than one occasion in your lifetime. Just as we can develop ears to recognize God's voice, discernment to know God's will is also available to the believer. I call it "the nod of God," when you feel a divine yes on the inside about something.

In Numbers 22, Balak tried to bribe Balaam, the prophet, to curse the Israelites. Balaam asked God if he should do it. When God told him no, Balak tempted Balaam with more money. A word to the wise: never move simply for more money. Balaam went back to prayer and asked God a second time to let him curse Israel. No matter how much money was involved, God would not change His mind.

Balaam, who I'm sure could have used the cash, was trying to talk God into doing his will instead of doing God's will.

This reminds me of how many people make decisions that do not have the nod of God accompanying them. They try to get God to bless the decisions or relationships when He has already said, "No, I don't believe that choice is right for you. I have someone or something better for you." Like Balaam, we sometimes go back to God, trying to change His mind. But God has made clear, *"For I am the LORD, I change not"* (Malachi 3:6 KJV). If God doesn't change, guess who *is* going to have to change?

Too often, we fail to ask God how He feels about our relationships, our financial investments, and the major decisions we make. I once wanted to buy a house in a great subdivision. I could just see our family living there, but when I prayed about the house, it seemed as though heaven's phone number was unlisted. Even though I told God what a good buy the house was, and what a great investment it would be for us, I could not get the nod of God to purchase that house. I might add that my wife sided with God and did not think the house was right for us either.

I kept going back day after day and asking God in prayer for peace about buying the home, but I just couldn't get a peace about it. Disappointed, I passed on purchasing the house. A few months later, I learned it was badly in need of major reconstruction. If I had not listened to the voices of God and my wife, that house would have cost me tens of thousands of dollars.

Proverbs 3:6 says, *"In all your ways acknowledge Him, and He shall direct your paths."* Your part is to acknowledge Him; His part is to direct your path. You may really want to buy that new car or house, but pray about it first and wait for the nod of God. Here's a tough question to ask yourself whenever you bring a decision before God: *are you willing to hear Him say no?*

Balaam kept asking God repeatedly to let him go, until God said, in effect, "All right, if you want to go, then go." It reminds me of my seven-year-old asking, "Daddy, can I go outside and play?" I say, "No, it's bad weather outside; you can't go." Five minutes later, he is back, pleading, "Daddy, Daddy, can I go now? Can I? Huh? Please, please, Daddy." At some point, I get so worn down and so tired of being asked, that I say, in frustration, "If you want to go so badly, then go." In reality, I'm not giving my permission; what I'm really doing is saying, "I dare you." I know that if he goes out in bad weather, he will suffer the consequences. He'll probably catch a cold.

> If you persist without the nod of God, He may let you have it— literally.

In the same way, God said to Balaam, "If you want to go, if you insist on going over My will, then go." Here's a frightening truth: there comes a time when, if you keep on stubbornly persisting about something that does not have the nod of God, He might just let you have it—literally. This always leads you down a painful road.

Balaam rode off on his donkey to curse Israel, but God put an angel in his path to stop Him. Balaam's donkey saw the angel in the middle of the road, but the prophet didn't. Sometimes, we can't see what we should, but God is gracious enough to surround us with those who can, until we can see it for ourselves. Have you ever been so headstrong, so outside of the will of God, that nobody could reason with you? The donkey was Balaam's friend, but Balaam beat the animal mercilessly because it would not continue to support him in going against God's will. Then, God supernaturally opened the mouth of the donkey and allowed it to speak to Balaam.

This had to be the world's most unusual conversation. Can you imagine these two donkeys talking to one another? One of them was a four-legged donkey, and the other was a two-legged donkey. The strange thing was, the four-legged donkey was the smarter of the two.

Balaam continued to kick and beat the donkey. In reality, he should have been kissing that donkey because it was trying to save his life. When we are stubborn and out of God's will, sometimes we kick and mistreat the well-intentioned. Young people kick their parents and embrace destructive friendships. Husbands and wives kick their spouses while they embrace destructive and divisive relationships.

Eventually, Balaam saw why the donkey was trying to turn him around. When you go in a direction that does not have the nod of God, sooner or later, you will see that God's way was the right way. You should immediately double back, swallow some pride, and thank all the people who had the courage to tell you the truth. Even when you were blinded by lust or self-ishness, God was faithful to put people in your path who tried to stop you from walking off that cliff.

I don't want to be like Balaam, a fool on a mule on the road to destruction. If I'm getting ready to mess up my life, I want God to stop me. When you wait for the nod of God before acting, it's like an early warning system that detects the enemy's mines and missiles before they are visible to the natural eye. From years of experience, I have learned to heed God's warnings. Every time I have brushed them off as merely being a case of indigestion or a mere coincidence, I have regretted it later. When you're about to make a major decision and you feel a "check in your spirit," or have a sense that something is wrong, you better heed the warning and wait for the nod of God.

When you have God's approval on your decisions, He will provide everything you need to do His will. Don't ask how much it costs; ask if God wants it done. If it's God will, then it's God's bill! Where God guides, He also provides. What God initiates, He will orchestrate. John 10:14 says, *"I know My sheep, and am known by My own."* His sheep recognize and follow the familiar voice of their Shepherd. They refuse to follow a stranger's voice.

How do the sheep know the Shepherd's voice? Through daily communion with the Shepherd. We must cultivate the ability to discern the voice of the Holy Spirit. When our relationship is distant, His voice seems muted. However, God will always hear us when we call, no matter how far away we've wandered. I know the voice of my children. I can be at a busy mall and hear other voices all around me, but when I hear one of my children say "Daddy," even in the midst of all the clutter, I instantly recognize that voice.

RACING AHEAD OR BEING LED

The problem is, we don't spend enough time with God to recognize His voice when He speaks. You cannot raise a family successfully without the voice of God leading you in wisdom. You cannot run a Christian business without the voice of God giving you direction. There is a vast difference between being led and racing ahead. When we don't hear Him, we find ourselves running at breakneck speed, confused and unproductive, always pushing and driving.

Are you racing ahead or are you being led? Your spirit wants to lead you; your flesh wants to race ahead like a toddler loose in a parking lot. The flesh thrives on noise, activity, competition, and busyness; the spirit thrives on silence, stillness, solitude, and Scripture. *"Be still, and know that I am God"* (Psalm 46:10).

A few years ago I participated in a mission trip to the Ukraine, where our church supports an orphanage in Kiev. While touring the orphanage I noticed a beautiful little eight-year-old girl. She stuck to me like glue. Every time I preached in the city at different churches, if she was there, she would come up and give me a hug. She truly captured my heart.

> The flesh thrives on noise and busyness; the spirit thrives on stillness and Scripture.

I went home and told my wife about her. I showed her pictures and, after much prayer and seeking God's will, we decided to pursue adopting the child. We were told it would be a relatively quick and easy process. Nothing could have been further from the truth.

We made numerous attempts to work out the adoption, including trips to the Ukraine where we met with government officials. We used all the contacts we had in that nation, as well as contacts within the States, but to no avail. Nothing we did brought us any closer to adoption. After two and a half years of emotional highs and lows, we finally realized that we were racing ahead in our own desire, rather than being led by the Spirit of God. It was one of the most painful times in our family's history.

When you try to force things to happen, it's almost always a sign that you are racing ahead, and not being led. As Psalm 23:2 reminds us, *"He leads me beside the still waters."* The whole time we were trying to adopt the little girl, we didn't have peaceful, still waters in our home. We had turmoil and confusion. We may never fully understand everything that happened during that season of our lives, but we have realized that being led by God brings peace, while racing ahead based on our own will exhausts all our resources.

THE WORD OF GOD

Jesus spent much time alone with God. If it was that important to the Son of God, there are certainly times when we must be alone with God as well. One of my favorite singers and musicians is Jason Upton. His music is some of the most inspirational that I have ever heard. He and his band go to a monastery every year for three to four days to seek God. During those days, they fast from speech—no sound, no music, no noise at all. In the quiet, God begins to speak. The spirit, you see, thrives on solitude. The voice of God does not scream; it's a still, small voice. In order for you to hear Him, you must learn to get quiet in His presence. You won't learn anything while you're doing the talking.

Many will argue that listening for the voice of God is too hard. In my family, there are seven of us: my wife, four girls, my son, and me. Sometimes, meals can be chaos; bedtimes can be a battle; outings can become an ordeal, but they are all a necessary part of everyday life. Spending time with God, although it may be difficult at first, is also a necessary part of everyday life—and one that helps get you through the rest of the chaos.

You have to plan your time with God. Make plans after the kids go to sleep or before they get up. You need those times alone with God so He can speak to you. He will give you confirmation about His will for your life. In order to spend time consistently with God, I set a place and a time for prayer.

God guides us by His Word, which is relevant for all people. Every believer has a right to hear God. Not knowing the Word of God, however, can greatly hinder you from receiving His direction. Psalm 119:105 says, *"Your word is a lamp to my feet and a light to my path."* The Scriptures are the Word of God, which the Spirit of God thrives in. Pour over them, and the Word of God will cleanse you of the world's impurities, wash you clean, and make you more like Christ.

Psalm 32:8–9 says, *"I will instruct you and teach you in the way you should go; I will guide you with My eye. Do not be like the horse or like the mule, which have no understanding, which must be harnessed with bit and bridle, else they will not come near you."* Parents understand the power of eye contact with their children. If you can just catch their eye, it's like a telepathic communication. You know what's going on, what they're feeling, and what they're planning.

You can be led by God's eye or by the bit and bridle. Don't be like the horse or the mule that has to have a bit and a bridle. You're a sheep, not a stubborn mule. Learn to listen to His impressions and wait on the nod of God.

FORCING YOUR WILL

Have you ever tried to put a puzzle together? Sometimes, a puzzle piece can look right, but it doesn't fit properly. It has the right appearance, but it will not fit into the empty space without force. If you have ever tried to force a piece to fit a space for which it was not designed, you know just one misplaced piece destroys the finish. It causes other pieces to become disjointed, and it will leave a hole someplace else. Every piece of a puzzle is connected, just like the pieces of our lives. We were created for a particular purpose, and just one piece out of place can greatly affect all the other pieces of our lives.

Don't try to force things to fit. Wait on the nod of God. If you don't have His approval for the direction you're headed, don't force it. God holds the missing piece of the puzzle.

You see, God has a dilemma: He expects us to realize that He is God, that His ways are not our ways, and that His thoughts are not our thoughts. (See Isaiah 55:8.) God's greatest pleasure is to be trusted.

TWO EXTREMES

Beware of wandering toward two extremes when trying to discern the voice of God. The first extreme is over-rationalizing. This is where you only do what is completely logical. Every door must be opened and every question answered before you will make a move. We say to God, "You show first, and then I'll go." But God says to us, "You go, and I'll show." He implores us to *"walk by faith, not by sight"* (2 Corinthians 5:7).

The other extreme is mysticism. To err on this side is to completely ignore reality. Everything becomes "I just felt led," or "God told me." There is nothing wrong with feeling led by God, but too many people use this line as a shield against the advice of others. It signals the end of the conversation.

One of the problems with the SCUD missiles in the first Gulf War was that, even though they were high-powered weapons, nobody knew quite where they were going to land. Being high-powered but misguided can often cause more harm than good.

EXPERIENCING GOD'S GUIDANCE

There are seven ways in which the discerning believer can truly experience God's guidance and determine God's will.

1. Inner Convictions

On February 24, 1989, a United Airlines 747 took off from Honolulu, Hawaii, headed for Sydney, Australia. While in flight, the cargo door blew open, sending some of its passengers to a watery grave in the Pacific Ocean. A man named John was on that flight. He spoke about the incident at a Christian business luncheon at our church. He was sitting at the passenger door, when he distinctly heard a voice on the inside saying, "Move from where you are sitting." He delayed, but the inner voice spoke again saying, "Move now!" He moved into the back of the plane and, a few seconds later, there was a gaping hole where he had been sitting.

Miraculously, the pilots were able to land the plane, but unfortunately, several people lost their lives. Although we'll never know why, John's life was spared that day by listening to the voice of God. Through the Holy Spirit, you can know things that you didn't study or train for. You can gain insight into someone's character. You can have a direct line into the wisdom and knowledge of God Himself.

2. Scriptural Confirmation

Second Timothy 3:16 teaches, *"All Scripture is given by inspiration of God, and is profitable for doctrine, for reproof, for correction, for instruction in righteousness."* Just as a pilot trusts his instruments, God guides us as we trust in His Word and in His Spirit. A good pilot will tell you that when you are in a storm or fog, you must trust the gauges on the flight panel more than your eyesight. When the storm is raging, stick to the gauges! The same is true in spiritual storms. The Word of God, and His Holy Spirit, will deliver you through the dark clouds of life.

3. Prophetic Confirmation

Through the prophetic word of someone else, God can confirm what He has already spoken to your heart. Sometimes He will use prophetic preaching, and it will seem as though the minister has eavesdropped on your life. First Corinthians 12 speaks of the nine gifts of the Holy Spirit. Two of them, the gifts of prophecy and the discerning of spirits, can help you know the right direction from the wrong direction.

4. Godly Counsel

Proverbs 11:14 says, *"Where there is no counsel, the people fall; but in the multitude of counselors there is safety."* Psalm 1:1 says, *"Blessed is the man who walks not in the counsel of the ungodly."* Before you make any major decision in your life, open yourself up to feedback from experienced, wise, godly people whom you respect. They are not a substitute for God's voice, but they may help you discover or confirm His leadings.

5. Circumstances

If you are laid off from your job, God may be directing you to another place of employment. In this case, He isn't leading you through prophecy, an internal voice, or an angel, but through your circumstances. There are times when God will allow things to happen in your life in order to get you to move. For example, no money in your bank account may be God's way of urging you to get a job. We certainly are not to govern all of our decisions by circumstances. However, there are times when we must interpret the circumstances of our lives, and then determine what God wants us to do.

6. The Peace of God

"Let the peace of God rule in your hearts" (Colossians 3:15). Don't enter into a contract or make a decision that robs you of your peace. Even if everything looks good and sounds good, always apply the peace test. It may take some trial and error to master this one, but learning to trust that barometer in your heart will help you to avoid some future hardship.

7. Provision

Remember my little saying: "Where God guides, He provides." Where's the provision? This doesn't mean you'll never experience financial challenges, but it does mean that He has already made provision for the vision that He has been putting into motion. *"I have not seen the righteous forsaken, nor his descendants begging bread"* (Psalm 37:25).

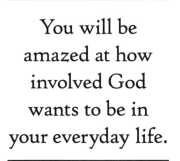

You will be amazed at how involved God wants to be in your everyday life.

In conclusion, I feel it is important for you to realize that, although God will choose any one of these ways to answer our prayers, He may use more than one to confirm His Word. God has told us that two or three witnesses will confirm His Word for us. (See Deuteronomy 19:15 and 2 Corinthians 13:1.) The bigger the decision, the more you will want to confirm His direction through these seven ways.

When you develop the ability to hear and discern God's voice, you will be amazed at how involved He wants to be in your everyday life. Ask God for His guidance; once you get the nod of God on your decisions, everything else will fall into place. *"And thine ears shall hear a word behind thee, saying, This is the way, walk ye in it"* (Isaiah 30:21 KJV).

There is a part of your brain called the reticular activating system. Have you ever bought a car thinking no one in your area owned one, but as soon as you drove off the lot, all you could see were cars just like yours? Suddenly, they seemed to be everywhere! Why didn't you notice them before? Because, after your purchase, your reticular activating system reprogrammed your brain to notice what you hadn't seen before—cars just like your new one.

Even as you're reading this book, God is activating a gift within your spirit called discernment. Maybe before you read this book, you didn't realize it was there. But from now on, it's going to be hard to miss the spiritual intuition God has given you.

I would like to pray into your life the principles we have learned so far:

> Father, in Jesus' name, I pray for the men and women of God who are reading these words. I pray that You will activate the gift of discernment in their lives. May You have full reign of their spirits so they can be stirred by Your Spirit, pressed by Your Spirit, bound by Your Spirit, and have rest in Your Spirit. I pray they will recognize the gentle whispers of the "moth" and be led by them. I pray for the nod of God to be on their every decision and relationship. I ask You to give them such a feel for the real that they will not miss Your purpose for any area of their lives. In Jesus' name I ask. Amen.

Part II

RIGHT PEOPLE, RIGHT PLACE, RIGHT PLAN

Chapter Four

RIGHT PEOPLE

There is a friend who sticks closer than a brother.
—Proverbs 18:24

Have you ever given your best in a relationship, and gotten the worst in return? Remember the lyrics of the popular country song, "Lookin' for Love," by Johnny Lee:

Lookin' for love in all the wrong places,
Lookin' for love in too many faces.

That has become a theme song for far too many people.

It's time to put a stop to getting burned. It's time to start enjoying the healthy, balanced relationships everyone wants and needs. God wants to help you make wise choices about the people you let into your life, from friendships to business partnerships to romance. Finding the proper people is an important part of determining God's will for your life.

If you have ever been used, abused, abandoned, or taken advantage of in a relationship, this chapter is for you. Too often, good people get entangled in bad relationships, with disastrous results.

CHARACTER DISCERNMENT

Character discernment is a valuable tool for avoiding toxic entanglements. It is a skill many of us lack. What is character discernment? It is simply the ability to find relationships that are good for you, and to avoid those that are not.

The apostle Paul said, *"You ran well. Who hindered you from obeying the truth?"* (Galatians 5:7). Notice he said *who*, not what. Romans 8:5 says, *"Those who live according to the flesh set their minds on the things of the flesh, but those who live according to the Spirit, the things of the Spirit."*

When some people come into your life, they don't just bring their bodies—they bring their spirits. There are two kinds of people: "flesh people" and "faith people."

Flesh people tear you down and feed your fears, while faith people build you up and feed your faith. Flesh people waste your time and drain your energy. Often, Christians find themselves in confusing relationships that drain them of their emotional energy and greatly reduce their effectiveness. Think of the personal pain that could be prevented if we knew how to avoid unhealthy relationships. This doesn't necessarily mean "flesh people" are bad people; it just means they don't belong in your inner circle. It also doesn't mean that you should shun such people; God wants us to love all those we come into contact with. But we have to make sure that we

> A warning sign of spiritual failure is isolation from other Christians and the house of God.

are surrounding ourselves with more people who fill our lives than drain our lives. One of the first warning signs of spiritual failure is when we begin to isolate ourselves from Christian friends and from the house of God.

Faith people are the kind who fill your life. They draw you closer to being the person God created you to be. They are the ones who will be lovingly honest with you. They are strong when you are weak.

If God wants to bless you, He will send a person; and if Satan wants to curse you, he will send a person. That's why, every day, we need to pray for 20/20 discernment in the world of the spirit to know the right people from the wrong people.

PAUL: THE PEOPLE WHO LIFT US UP

When Paul needed to be healed, whom did God send? Ananias was the right man in the right place at the right time. (See Acts 9:10–18.) That's what I call a "Kingdom Connection:" people God puts in your life who act like a bridge to get you where you're supposed to go. How would you like some Kingdom Connections in your life and career?

The early church rejected Paul because he had persecuted Christians before his conversion. The disciples were afraid of him, so God once again sent a person: Barnabas. Barnabas used his influence with the disciples to get Paul's foot in the door of the church.

When Paul was discouraged, God sent Titus to encourage him. Have you ever had a discouraging day until one person shared some kind words and completely changed your mood? In 2 Corinthians 7:6, Paul said, *"Nevertheless God, who comforts the downcast, comforted us by the coming of Titus."*

RUTH: THE PEOPLE WE MARRY

Marriage is one of the most important decisions you will ever make. It is a commitment for life. It affects every other area in your life: your future children, where you live, your finances, where you go to church, and so much more. God has a plan for the people you associate with in your dating life. You will be better off if you take the time to be sure that the one you marry is the one who is ordained by God.

Does God care if you are single, widowed, or divorced? Does He notice when everybody else goes home together, but you go home alone? You bet He notices! In the book of Ruth, we see the God who said, *"It is not good that man* [or woman] *should be alone"* (Genesis 2:18), step into the shadows of Ruth's life and give her a Kingdom Connection. Ruth's husband had died and she had little prospect of finding a good man. But God didn't send her a loser or a reject. He didn't send her a smooth-talking "player" who would break her heart. He sent her a man who was capable and could care for her. He sent her Boaz.

Boaz was a bit older than Ruth was, but he had enough money to make her comfortable. Notice the qualities that you should look for, or teach your children to look for, when trying to discern the right mate. Boaz was a stable man. He wasn't just out of prison or rehab. Nor was he lazy and unproductive.

Notice also that he was respectful to Ruth's relatives. He gave Ruth food to take home to her mother-in-law, Naomi. Boaz paid the bill; they didn't "go Dutch." These days, men don't seem to understand how to respect a woman and show respect to her parents. Ladies, if you are dating a guy who reluctantly pays for the meal on the date, but expects you to pay for the movie and the popcorn, then you're dating a dead-beat. Take notes here, gentlemen. Boaz was a man's man—a perceptive man, a sensitive man, a spiritual man, and a financially capable man. That's an equation that equals a *husband!*

When Ruth came home loaded with food, Naomi began to mentor her on how to conduct herself in a proper way. When Ruth wanted to know what she should do about this man showing her romantic interest, Naomi gave her some sound advice: *"Sit still, my daughter, until you know how the matter will turn out"* (Ruth 3:18). "Sit still and wait." In other words, "Let the man pursue you; don't pursue him." Today, the girl would call back in thirty minutes saying, "Do you remember me, Boaz? I met you in the field." The next morning she would be calling again. "Do you remember me? Can we go out on a date sometime?" Men lose respect for desperate women. Sitting still and waiting is the hardest thing to do. This actually means you will have to trust God in the matter. Even if you're camping out by the phone, waiting on him to call, don't let him know it. Sit still and wait! Ruth could have reacted selfishly and told old Naomi, "You don't know what you're talking about. Just because you lost your husband doesn't mean that I'm going to lose a chance at a second one." But she didn't. The Bible said she obeyed and respected Naomi's advice.

Boaz arranged a legal wedding and became her "kins-man-redeemer." They had a son named Obed. Obed had a son named Jesse. Jesse had a son named David, who became a king. David had a descendant named Mary. And Mary had a little child that she named Jesus.

Through Ruth's character discernment, God not only blessed her with a fantastic husband, but He also placed her in the genealogy of Jesus Christ. (See Matthew 1:5.)

JONAH: THE PEOPLE WHO TAKE US DOWN

We need God to restore discernment within us, so we can recognize the right people, the blessed people, the faith people, the Kingdom Connections He has for each one of us. But we also need discernment to recognize the wrong people.

God sent Jonah on a mission to Nineveh. But Jonah disobeyed God's will and headed in the opposite direction to Joppa, where he boarded a ship for Tarshish. During the voyage, the ship he was on ran into a storm that threatened to capsize it. Jonah 1:5 says, *"The mariners were afraid."* Many of us have heard the story of Jonah in sermons and Sunday school lessons, but have you ever stopped to consider the fact that there were other people besides Jonah on the boat about to lose their lives? All it takes is one rebellious, disobedient man to take a whole shipload of people down with him.

> One rebellious, disobedient man can take a whole shipload of people down with him.

This is an important lesson for those trying to learn discernment. There are times when you are not the problem. The problem may be the people with whom you're associating. The mariner's boat was taking on water, everyone on board was terrified for their very lives, and it wasn't their fault. They were in the wrong place, at the wrong time, with the wrong person—Jonah.

The mariners were feverishly crying out to their gods. They were casting off supplies, sacrificing their needs to lighten the load. But Scripture tells us that *"Jonah had gone down into the lowest parts of the ship, had lain down, and was fast asleep"* (Jonah

1:5). Sometimes, when your life is rocking and reeling in the storm, it's because of people to whom you have attached yourself!

Finally, the mariners woke Jonah from his sleep and asked him, *"What shall we do to you that the sea may be calm for us?"* (verse 11). Jonah answered them, *"Pick me up and throw me into the sea; then the sea will become calm for you. For I know that this great tempest is because of me"* (verse 12). Jonah knew he was the problem. So, why would he ask them to cast him over? Why not just jump off the boat?

Sometimes, rebels try to make you feel bad. If you have a forty-five-year-old son who won't get a job, is still living at home eating your food, and is not paying rent, then it's time to throw Jonah off the boat! When you do, don't be surprised if he tries to make you feel guilty for doing the right thing. I can just hear his pitiful words, "You're right; I know I should do better. I'll just find somewhere else to stay. I guess I could sleep at the bus station."

We can wander into storms simply by trying to help people by doing for them what they should be doing for themselves. If the mariners had not tossed Jonah off the boat, everyone would have perished. If you have people in your life who are using you for a free ride, they're not going to voluntarily jump off the boat. If you have relatives or friends who play on your conscience and goodwill to get you to pay their bills or give them money, do you think they're going to stop? If you have a husband who physically abuses you or has affairs on the side and you allow it, you are giving him a license to treat you like a dog.

The Bible says that before they threw Jonah off the boat, they tried rowing harder to bring the ship to land. We often try to work a problem harder because we are afraid of the decision we know we are going to have to make. We try so hard to reap success out of sin. Finally someone on the boat called a meeting. They took a vote and decided to throw Jonah off the boat. I'm sure the mariners felt bad about it, but they knew that, if they didn't, they were not going to make it to the other side. The Bible continues, *"So they picked up Jonah and threw him into the sea, and the sea ceased from its raging"* (Jonah 1:15). As soon as you get the wrong people out of your boat, your storm will cease. You will experience a great calm. Some of you need to throw some Jonahs off your boat!

> When you allow the wrong people in your life, you're keeping them from God's best.

If you throw a Jonah off your boat, remember that God is still there for him. When they threw Jonah off the boat, God had already prepared a great fish to swallow him and spit him back onto the shore so he could travel on to Nineveh, his intended destination. When you allow the wrong people in your life, you're not helping them—you may be keeping them from what God has prepared for them.

Ask God to reveal the Jonahs in your life who are rocking the boat. Pray for the wisdom and courage to "throw" them and all their baggage off your boat! Sometimes, you have to do what is best for you and trust God to take care of the other person.

As soon as Jonah was off the boat, the mariners began to worship God. (See Jonah 1:16.) You cannot worship God as you ought to as long as there are toxic relationships and turmoil all around. Whatever is stealing your peace and rocking your boat, whatever is taking your smile away, reach down, pick it up, and throw it overboard. Then do what the mariners did—start worshipping God.

WHO'S YOUR MENTOR?

One of the secrets of success for some of the great Bible heroes was their mentors. If you don't have a godly mentor in your life, you need to ask Him to put one there. When He does, don't hang back and wait for the person to approach you; you might need to ask him or her to mentor you. Joshua was always there, hanging out around Moses. Elisha's success was found in his relationship with Elijah. He spent hours and hours learning from the wise old prophet.

The apostle Paul called Timothy *"a true son in the faith"* (1 Timothy 1:2). Timothy was one of the youngest apostles in the Bible. How did he succeed at such a young age? He literally sat at the feet of the great apostle Paul and caught his spirit.

Jesus spent three and a half years of His life in ministry. Most of His time was not with the crowds, or with rich and influential leaders, but with twelve men into whom He poured His life and wisdom. He would speak in parables to the crowds of people, then He would explain and elaborate with the disciples. These men became the building blocks of His church.

Mentors expose you to new orbits of ministry, new habits, and new levels of expectation. Ask the weight lifter or the track-and-field high jumper what a coach does for them. If you want to be the best, the mentor will keep raising the bar, asking for a little more effort and for better results, and teaching you to expect more from yourself.

At times, mentors may even seem cruel and inconsiderate, but if you want to be a winner, their coaching can urge you to the top. Proverbs 27:6 says, *"Faithful are the wounds of a friend, but the kisses of an enemy are deceitful.*" It's a great day when God gives you someone who loves you enough to put you under a little pressure so you can be conformed into the image of Jesus Christ and reach your highest potential.

BEWARE FALSE BRETHREN

If you have spent your life gravitating toward all the wrong people, I have good news for you. God will bring the right people and toss out the wrong people. But when He does, don't return to the wrong people. *"Every branch in Me that does not bear fruit He takes away"* (John 15:2). That does not mean they're inferior and you're superior; it just means they are not a part of God's plan for your life. Like Jonah, God has a different plan, a different course, for them. But if you insist on grafting them into your life, God may have to do relational surgery and prune them out.

Unfortunately, such false brethren can sometimes be found within your own family, where it is hard to prune them out. At family gatherings, they often bring condemnation. It was only when the prodigal son failed that he realized what his older brother was made of. Upon his return and repentance, his father did not bring up the sins of the prodigal. It was his elder brother who pointed his finger and condemned the prodigal son to his father. (See Luke 15:11–32.)

Joseph discovered that false brethren never celebrate your dream. Instead of living in God's land of unlimited favor, they live in a "zero sum" mentality where for you to win, they must lose. Your gain is their loss. If you receive blessing, they believe somehow there are less blessings available for them. Joseph's brothers couldn't stand their father's favor toward the young lad so they threw him into a pit and sold him into slavery. (See Genesis 37:24.)

Some people bless you when they come into your life; some people bless you when they exit your life. There are many good people out there. *"There is a friend who sticks closer than a brother"* (Proverbs 18:24). Use every ounce of wisdom and discernment to find such people. If someone is destructive or producing bad fruit in your life, be careful. Keep looking, praying, and seeking until you find the right people, who draw you closer to being the person God intended you to be.

Chapter Five

RIGHT PLACE

And He has made from one blood
every nation of men to dwell on all the face of the earth,
and has determined their preappointed times
and the boundaries of their dwellings.

—Acts 17:26

Over twelve years ago, God began to speak to me about this amazing gift of discernment. I had a dream one Saturday night that was so vivid I will never forget it. I dreamed I was attending the funeral of a child. When I walked up to the little casket and looked in, I was devastated to see Caressa, my three-year-old daughter, lying lifeless in the coffin. Immediately, I woke up from the dream and awakened my wife. We both began to pray for our family. We wept as the strong presence of the Lord entered our bedroom.

The next morning, still shaken by this experience, I went to church to preach. I preached a sermon I titled "Cancel the Devil's Assignment." At the end of the message, I tearfully told the congregation about my dream. I explained how I believed God was warning me that Satan had targeted our children at a young age, but through the blood of Jesus Christ, we could cancel the devil's assignment in their lives. It was one of the most moving services I've ever taken part in, as fathers and mothers began to cry out to God on behalf of their families.

This is where the story takes a dramatic turn. Our family had planned to go on vacation to Disney World in Florida the next day. For some strange reason, my wife begged me to leave after the morning services ended. She kept on pleading with me, "Let's go one day early so we can go to SeaWorld tomorrow." SeaWorld hadn't even been on our itinerary, but I consented, and we arrived in Florida one day early.

The next morning, we took our two daughters to SeaWorld. It was a beautiful, sunny day as we waited for the ski show to begin in the uncovered, five-thousand-seat stadium. Out of nowhere, a huge, dark storm cloud emerged and covered the park. The wind picked up drastically. We heard a clap of thunder when, suddenly, right before our eyes, a streak of lightning hit the top of a nearby hotel, setting it on fire. Panic-stricken, five thousand people rushed up the steps of the stadium, seeking shelter from the storm.

Total chaos ensued. Cherise grabbed the diaper bag and accessories while I snatched one of the girls. Our youngest daughter walked up the steps herself. By the time we neared the top of the stadium, thunder and lightning were all around us. Both of our girls were hysterical. To be honest, so was I. Never before had I encountered anything like this. The strong winds triggered my mind to watch for a tornado. When we reached the top of the steps, it was so crowded that Cherise quickly turned to pick up Caressa. But, as she reached for her, Caressa ran right past her to a total stranger standing nearby. The stranger, a twenty-six-year-old woman, reached down and picked up our daughter without hesitation. Caressa wrapped her arms around the young lady's neck and wouldn't let her go.

Of all our children, Caressa was by far the clingiest to her mother; she would never go into a stranger's arms. She always wanted her mother or me to hold her. If she didn't know someone, she wouldn't give them the time of day.

Yet, as Cherise began to plead with her to come into her arms, Caressa wouldn't even acknowledge Cherise or me. She just clung to this woman with all of her might. The lady began to cry—not a tear or two, but uncontrollable sobbing—as she held our three-year-old daughter.

Cherise turned to me and whispered, "Jentezen, do something. This lady is acting weird, and she has our child." I noticed the young woman's mother and father standing beside her, and I saw that her mother was also crying. Now we were totally confused.

My wife gently asked the woman's mother, "Why is everyone crying?"

She responded, "You don't understand. Your daughter is a little angel sent from God to us today."

As the storm started to recede, she began to explain.

"Two months ago, my daughter's three-year-old child died of congestive heart failure in the middle of the night. This is the first time we have been able to get our daughter out of her bedroom because she has been so devastated with grief. She's been blaming God for taking her little girl."

The young woman continued to weep, holding our child tightly as Caressa continued to cling to her. Cherise and I were moved to tears. As the crowd began to break up and return to their seats, many people were staring at us, wondering what was going on.

I asked the young mother who was holding Caressa to listen to me. I said, "I'm a minister, and what I'm about to tell you is on video if you don't believe it. This past Saturday night, I had a dream. In the dream, God let me feel your grief. I saw my three-year-old in a coffin. I have never felt grief like that in my life. I went to church the next day and told my congregation about seeing my child in a coffin. The reason we're here today at SeaWorld is because my wife decided she wanted to come one day early. Now, I know why. God wanted you to know your precious daughter is with Him in heaven."

I went on to tell her that our three-year-old has never run into the arms of a complete stranger. "This is a sign from God to you of how much He loves you." I explained to her that King David, in the Bible, also lost a son and said, *"Can I bring him back again? I shall go to him, but he shall not return to me"* (2 Samuel 12:23). I told the woman, "You must determine, even though you can't bring back your child, that someday you will go to the place where your child has gone."

The whole family tearfully prayed with us. God's healing presence was so strong, we felt like we were standing on holy ground. While the young mother still held Caressa, our daughter began to play with a little pearl necklace around the mother's neck. The grieving mother had placed a similar necklace around the neck of her child as she lay in her casket. The woman unhooked the necklace and snapped it around Caressa's neck. In doing so, she was essentially letting go of her little girl and placing her in God's loving hands.

The young woman told us that this experience had restored her faith in God. After we all cried and prayed, it was time to go our separate ways. When we tried to pry Caressa from her arms, she threw a fit because she wanted to stay with the young woman. To us, that was stranger than anything else.

My wife and I will never forget that family standing and weeping as we walked away, with Caressa reaching back toward that mother. Think of the measures to which God will go just to tell us He loves us when we are hurting!

If we are hurting, He hurts, too. *"For we do not have a High Priest who cannot sympathize with our weaknesses"* (Hebrews 4:15). Jesus allowed Himself to be forsaken by God so He could say, "I know, I've been there." Our God knows the pain of loss. He is moved by the same things that distress us.

> Suffering never leaves you where it finds you; you either become bitter or better.

Suffering never leaves you where it finds you; you either become bitter or better. It either turns you into a miserable complainer, or conforms you into the image of Jesus Christ. God loved that young mother so much that He gave me a dream, rearranged our schedule, gave my wife discernment to insist on leaving early, and even used my three-year-old daughter's affections to move her to the right place at the right time—the arms of a broken, hurting woman.

Think of it. Out of thousands of people in that stadium, God put us in the right place, at the right time.

PROPER PLACEMENT

One of God's primary purposes for your life is proper placement. Being in the right place at the right time is an important key to discovering God's will for your life. In Genesis 1, God created a place and He created Adam; in Genesis 2, God planted Adam into the proper place, a garden.

What does this tell you about God and His will for your life?

1. God doesn't leave you where He finds you.

2. God has a proper placement for you.

The owner of the first "placement service" in the world was God. Paul wrote, *"God has set the members, each one of them, in the body just as He pleased"* (1 Corinthians 12:18). God comes to you right where you are and gives you a purpose, a mission, and a place. God gave Adam a place of employment before He gave him a wife. If you're a single woman, you shouldn't consider marrying any man who doesn't have his place of employment—a job.

Proper placement profoundly affects your future in seven ways:

1. It releases supernatural provision in your life.

2. It provides protection.

3. It demands the death of pride.

4. It is often preceded by a season of discomfort.

5. It releases the glory of God on your life.

6. It prevents exposure to sinful situations and temptations you would encounter if improperly placed.

7. It can help you to avoid future problems.

1. IT RELEASES SUPERNATURAL PROVISION

First Kings 17:3–4 describes supernatural provision:

Get away from here and turn eastward, and hide by the Brook Cherith, which flows into the Jordan. And it will be that you shall drink from the brook, and I have commanded the ravens to feed you there.

During a famine, God gave Elijah clear instruction, saying, in effect, "Go to Cherith. I have commanded the ravens to feed you *there*." God told Elijah that if he moved to the right place, supernatural provision *would* show up. Divine supply follows divine placement. If Elijah had been any other place but the right place, the ravens would not have fed him. God holds your place of supernatural provision—God has a "there" for you!

Just about the time Elijah thought he had God all figured out, suddenly the brook dried up and the ravens stopped bringing food. I once preached a sermon called, "What to Do When the Brook Goes Dry and the Birds Won't Fly!" In it, I explained that the only reason God lets the brook dry up is that He wants to drive you back to your source. We are to seek God's face, not His hand. We want a handout, but God wants a face-off.

> We are to seek God's face, not His hand. We want a handout but God wants a face-off.

Don't fall in love with a method and forget that God is your source. The brook wasn't Elijah's source; God was. We get married to a method, anchored to a memory, but we must be open to change. When the Holy Spirit wants to do a new thing, we have to get away from the old wineskins. In this case, God gave Elijah a new plan, *"Go to Zarephath....I have commanded a widow there to provide for you"* (1 Kings 17:9).

My wife has her own contracting company. She has such a great gift in this area that her talent has blessed us financially. In fact, the first home that we owned was one that she built. We lived with her parents for four years while saving all the money we could. Finally, we had enough money to buy an empty lake property that Cherise had found in Gainesville, Georgia. She really felt that we needed to stretch our resources and try to purchase it. We paid $50,000 for the lot, exhausting all the money we had. We secured a $130,000 loan for the home, and Cherise built a beautiful home on the lake. We lived in it for a year and then sold it for $389,000.

The story gets better. She later found another lot on the lake in a beautiful neighborhood. This lot was a whopping $180,000! That was almost the entire profit from the sale of our first home. I felt the lot was too costly and that we would never get our money out of it. Still, her amazing financial discernment caused her to persist. She said, "I can build a home on this lot and make a fortune." Thankfully, I listened to her. Today, the lot alone is valued at over one million dollars.

Through the years, my wife has had an uncanny ability to make wise financial investments in the area of real estate. Regretfully, I have not always listened to her. Consequently, we've missed some incredible financial blessings. But I've learned that one of my wife's strong points is in business, so I'm glad to take a backseat to her in this area.

Discern the place of blessing for your life. If God says, "I'll bless you 'there,'" and you insist on staying "here," then you're going to miss His provision. Everything was dependent upon Elisha being in the right location.

When Ruth was looking for a place of provision, she

expressed her desire to her mother-in-law, Naomi. *"Please let me go to the field, and glean heads of grain after him in whose sight I may find favor"* (Ruth 2:2). You don't want to work in just any field. Pray for discernment that will lead you into an occupational field where you will find the favor of your employer. The place God has for you will be a place of influence, favor, and prosperity.

Sometimes, the place God sends you won't appear to be a place of blessing. When Ruth found the right field in which to work, she labored in only a remote corner of it. Later, she was promoted from working in that insignificant corner to owning the entire field! But, her promotion was contingent upon finding the right place of employment.

Are you in the right place, or are you leaning on an old plow, afraid to let go?

In 2 Chronicles 7:12, God said to Solomon, *"I have heard your prayer, and have chosen this place for Myself as a house of sacrifice."* Oh, the potential of a chosen place. If you are in such a place, don't leave it. If you are not, don't stay where you are another day longer than you have to. In Exodus 33:21, God said to Moses, *"Here is a place by Me, and you shall stand on the rock."* There is a place reserved for you by God. If you will move there, God will supernaturally provide all you need to do His will.

2. IT PROVIDES A PLACE OF PROTECTION

A wrong place is any place where you know your Christian walk is compromised. When you stay out of the wrong places, you protect your integrity. Any place that Christ Himself would not go is the wrong environment. A good rule to follow is, "If Christ wouldn't, you shouldn't!"

In the cool of the day, Adam and Eve would walk with God in the garden of Eden. When they were with God, Satan never showed up. He approached Eve when she was absent from God's presence.

As long as Peter stayed near Jesus' side, he was strong in faith; but when he was alone—absent from the presence of Jesus—he warmed his hands by the wrong fire and denied Christ three times. (See John 18:17–18, 25–27.)

There is protection in His presence. Don't stray too far from the body of Christ, which is the church, or you'll become easy prey for the enemy.

3. It Demands the Death of Pride

Proper placement demands the death of pride. This is a tough one! Pride is one of the main obstacles blocking your move to the right place. When we are puffed up with pride, we say things like, "Well, I'm not going to work there. I'm better than they are."

Elijah was a great and mighty man of God. He was a big, strong prophet who killed four hundred fifty prophets of Baal and called down fire from heaven. But in 1 Kings, God instructed him to seek help at the home of a widow: *"I have commanded a widow there to provide for you"* (1 Kings 17:9). This would have been a perfect time for pride to swell within Elijah. He could have said, "I'm not going to lower myself by asking for help from that woman." But he didn't allow pride to keep him from the right place.

Men can learn a lot from their wives, but pride won't let them say, "I was wrong; you were right." Often, finding your proper placement demands the death of personal pride.

4. It Is Often Preceded by a Season of Discomfort

Proper placement is often preceded by a season of discomfort. The reason is simple: until your misery factor exceeds your fear factor, you won't change. We prize security.

When a mother eagle wants her eaglets to learn how to fly, she begins to tear up the nest. She removes the animal fur to expose the briars and thorns. Suddenly, the nest isn't such a comfortable place anymore, so the eaglets swiftly desire to stretch their wings and learn to soar. You'll never fly if you're too comfortable. You will never change that which you are willing to tolerate. God has a way of making us move out. It's called discomfort.

5. It Releases the Glory of God

Proper placement releases the glory of God on your life. In the book of Exodus, God told Moses how to construct the tabernacle:

I have put wisdom in the hearts of all who are gifted artisans, that they may make all that I have commanded you: the tabernacle of meeting, the ark of the Testimony and the mercy seat that is on it, and all the furniture of the tabernacle; the table and its utensils, the pure gold lampstand with all its utensils, the altar of incense, the altar of burnt offering with all its utensils, and the laver and its base; the garments of ministry, the holy garments for Aaron the priest and the garments of his sons, to minister as priests, and the anointing oil and sweet incense for the holy place. According to all that I have commanded you they shall do.

(Exodus 31:6–11)

God gave specific dimensions, colors, and furniture place-ment, and even specified the garments that were to be worn there. They did exactly what God said, and the results were spectacular. *"Then the cloud covered the tabernacle of meeting, and the glory of the LORD filled the tabernacle"* (Exodus 40:34). In 2 Chronicles, after Solomon completed the more permanent temple and all the furniture was properly placed, the Scripture says, *"Fire came down from heaven and consumed the burnt offer-ing and the sacrifices; and the glory of the LORD filled the temple"* (2 Chronicles 7:1). The right place and the right job release the glory of God upon our lives.

6. IT PREVENTS EXPOSURE TO SINFUL SITUATIONS AND TEMPTATION

If you will listen to and obey God's voice, His glory will be your reward. Failing to do so may subject you to sinful situa-tions and temptations.

The first words God spoke to Adam after he sinned referred to Adam's location. *"Then the LORD God called to Adam and said to him, 'Where are you?'"* (Genesis 3:9). Adam's sin drove him out of the place specifically prepared for him.

Lot was the nephew of Abram, but he left his uncle and moved to Sodom. What was he doing living in Sodom? Lot saw an opportunity to get rich, but eventually lost his wife in the process because he wasn't where he was supposed to be.

7. IT CAN HELP YOU TO AVOID FUTURE PROBLEMS

Living within the proper placement of God can make all the difference between a life of blessing and a life of sorrow. If you live in the right city, go to the right church, find the right job, hang out with the right people, and marry the right spouse, many potential problems will be averted.

How do you discover the right place? Repent, pray, and expect divine guidance.

Repent; stop doing your own thing.

Psalm 92:13 says, *"Those who are planted in the house of the Lord shall flourish in the courts of our God."* Don't be a tumble-weed Christian, fruitless and rootless, blowing in and out of churches. Get rooted and grounded in the right church.

The prodigal son finally came to his senses and realized that he was in the wrong place, living in a pigpen, when he said, *"I will arise and go to my father"* (Luke 15:18). He was saying, in effect, "I'm leaving the wrong place and going back to the right place." (See Luke 15:11–32.)

Pray for God's timing and God's place.

We are not asking for something that God doesn't know. Acts 17:26 says, *"And He has made from one blood every nation of men to dwell on all the face of the earth, and has determined their preappointed times and the boundaries of their dwellings."* According to Scripture, God assigns a place for you and sets a time for you to be there.

Expect divine guidance.

Missing God's will produces severe consequences. It is my belief that you are safer fighting in a war within the will of God than spending a day at the beach outside of the will of God.

It has been said, "If God closes one door, He will open another one." That is true, but you don't want to hang out very long in the hallway. When God closes one door and you're standing in the hallway waiting for the next door to open, then

73

yearn, hunger for His divine guidance. *"The steps of a good man are ordered by the LORD"* (Psalm 37:23).

The voice of discernment God has placed within you will lead you to the right places where you will make Kingdom Connections (the right people, at the right place, at the right time). Learn to listen to your inner voice of discernment in order to release supernatural provision into your life and the lives of those you meet.

God has a SeaWorld assignment for you. Someone out there is in his or her dark night of the soul. People are counting on you to be sensitive enough to God's leading that you will be in the right place at the right time so He can use you to shine His light into their darkness.

Chapter Six

Right Plan

For I know the thoughts that I think toward you,
says the LORD, thoughts of peace and not of evil,
to give you a future and a hope.
—Jeremiah 29:11

There is a right plan. One idea from God can change your life. Thomas Edison had one idea, and today we have the electric lightbulb. The Wright brothers had one idea, and now we have aviation. Bill Gates had one idea, and today we have the personal computer. There are "good ideas," and there are "God ideas." The Holy Spirit wants you to discern the difference between the two.

PRAY FOR A MIRACLE—GET A PLAN

Perhaps, today, you need a miracle, for you or your family. When you ask God for a miracle, He will often give you a set of instructions—a plan. He rarely releases a miracle without a plan. Too often we pray and then sit back and wait for God to do miracles. If you read your Bible, however, you'll find it doesn't work that way. You want a miracle? You're going to receive a set of instructions—a plan.

When Joshua needed a miracle of conquest, God gave him a plan.

> *You shall march around the city, all you men of war; you shall go all around the city once. This you shall do six days. And seven priests shall bear seven trumpets of rams' horns before the ark. But the seventh day you shall march around the city seven times, and the priests shall blow the trumpets. It shall come to pass, when they make a long blast with the ram's horn, and when you hear the sound of the trumpet, that all the people shall shout with a great shout; then the wall of the city will fall down flat. And the people shall go up every man straight before him.* (Joshua 6:3–5)

God said, in effect, "Here's the plan: march six times over six days, and on the seventh day, march seven times. Then blow the horns and shout—and the walls will fall." Joshua obeyed, and God's plan brought the walls of Jericho down.

When Naaman sought a miracle of healing for his leprosy, God provided a plan through the prophet Elisha. *"Go and wash in the Jordan seven times, and your flesh shall be restored to you, and you shall be clean"* (2 Kings 5:10). That simple set of instructions from God brought a miraculous healing to Naaman's body. (See verse 14.)

Before Samson was ever born, God appeared to his mother and said, *"For behold, you shall conceive and bear a son. And no razor shall come upon his head, for the child shall be a Nazarite to God from the womb; and he shall begin to deliver Israel out of the hand of the Philistines"* (Judges 13:5). God already had a miraculous and detailed plan for his life before the boy was ever born.

Similar stories are told in the New Testament. In the first chapter of Luke, Elizabeth and Zacharias were told by the angel of God they would have a son. Very little was left to chance.

> *Your wife Elizabeth will bear you a son, and you shall call his name John. And you will have joy and gladness, and many will rejoice at his birth. For he will be great in the sight of the Lord, and shall drink neither wine nor strong drink. He will also be filled with the Holy Spirit, even from his mother's womb. And he will turn many of the children of Israel to the Lord their God. He will also go before Him in the spirit and power of Elijah, "to turn the hearts of the fathers to the children," and the disobedient to the wisdom of the just, to make ready a people prepared for the Lord.*
>
> (Luke 1:13–17)

Once again, the plan of God came with a name and an assignment, before Elizabeth was ever pregnant with John the Baptist, their miracle child.

At the wedding in Cana, when Mary asked her Son for a miracle of provision, Jesus gave a plan. Mary had enough experience with the plans of God that she knew what to do.

> *His mother said to the servants, "Whatever He says to you, do it." Now there were set there six waterpots of stone, according to the manner of purification of the Jews, containing twenty or thirty gallons apiece. Jesus said to them, "Fill the waterpots with water." And they filled them up to the brim. And He said to them, "Draw some out now, and take it to the master of the feast." And they took it.*
>
> (John 2:5–8)

The water blushed in the presence of its Creator, turning into wine of the highest caliber. (See John 2:8–10.) When you ask God for a miracle, He connects your miracle result to a miracle plan.

KNOW THE SOURCE

Jeremiah 29:11 says, *"For I know the thoughts that I think toward you, says the LORD, thoughts of peace and not of evil, to give you a future and a hope."* God made you for a purpose. When you don't know why something is made, you can easily abuse it. Don't ask the creation what its purpose is; ask its Creator.

Some of you may be thinking, *You don't know where I came from, the things I've done. You don't know my parents. I came from an illegitimate background.*

That doesn't matter to God.

Here's what you need to understand: *"Before I formed you in the womb I knew you; before you were born I sanctified you; I ordained you"* (Jeremiah 1:5). You don't come from a background. You don't come from your parents. You may have come *through* them, but you didn't come *from* them. You come from God. Your assignment can't be messed up by your circumstances.

Ephesians 2:10 reminds us, *"For we are His workmanship, created in Christ Jesus for good works, which God prepared beforehand that we should walk in them."* When you were created, God encoded you for an assignment, and He gave you the power to get it done. The enemy's job is to pull us out of that divine assignment, out of the will of God.

Every assignment has a birthplace. Destiny is reached by discerning those transitional moments when God sends you His road map leading to your purpose.

The church I pastor, Free Chapel, has been in existence for over fifty years. The former pastor, Roy Wellborn, scheduled me to come preach a revival every year when I was a full-time evangelist. The last time I preached for Pastor Wellborn, it was scheduled nine months in advance. Just prior to the date, however, he became ill, was hospitalized, and passed away. He died on Friday night; I was to preach that Sunday.

The congregation loved Pastor Wellborn. They were devastated at his passing. You can imagine how inadequate I felt standing in the pulpit two days after his death—the pulpit this beloved man had faithfully filled for over thirty years. As soon as the morning's service ended, they rolled the coffin in and held Pastor Wellborn's memorial service.

> **God's plan often comes through unexpected events that force you in a direction you never would have gone.**

At that time, I had no idea that I was there by the divine plan of almighty God. I'm sure that when Pastor Wellborn scheduled me to preach in his church, he had no idea he would be in heaven that very week, or that God had already chosen me as his replacement.

God really does have a marvelous plan for our lives. Pray for special insight into His plans for your life. You will discover that *"eye has not seen, nor ear heard, nor have entered into the heart of man the things which God has prepared for those who love Him"* (1 Corinthians 2:9).

GOD'S UNEXPECTED PLAN

God's plan for your life will often come through unexpected events that force you in a direction you never would have gone. Esther experienced the providential leading of God that gave her assignment a "birthplace."

The book of Esther opens with a wild seven-day party in the king's palace. King Ahasuerus asked all of his council of warlords to join him on his next military expedition. He was hungry for power. In order to sell his idea, he decided to "wine and dine" his warlords for seven days.

At the end of seven days of partying, the epitome of the seduction was flaunting the best-looking women in the king's harem in dance. These shapely, beautiful women danced before the drunken warlords, ensuring that they would be ready to follow the king wherever he led them into battle.

As the icing on the cake, the custom was to bring the queen out to dance in order to close the deal. There was nothing unusual about the king asking Queen Vashti to dance; what was unusual was for her to refuse. When the queen failed to appear, one of his warlords exclaimed,

> *The queen's behavior will become known to all women, so that they will despise their husbands in their eyes, when they report, "King Ahasuerus commanded Queen Vashti to be brought in before him, but she did not come." This very day the noble ladies of Persia and Media will say to all the king's officials that they have heard of the behavior of the queen. Thus there will be excessive contempt and wrath.*
>
> (Esther 1:17–18)

Greatly embarrassed, King Ahasuerus decided to get rid of his queen. Suddenly, here was a king without a queen. In order to find a new queen, the palace announced a "national beauty contest." As a result, one hundred twenty-seven women were selected from the provinces for the king's consideration. Esther, a young orphan girl, was chosen as one of them.

Queen Vashti's fatal attitude set the stage for the higher purpose of God. Sometimes, when things happen you can't explain, these paradoxical occurrences tell us somebody else is in charge. As Christians, we don't believe things happen by chance; instead, we believe God has a plan for our lives. It's interesting how God often seems to use people with disadvantaged backgrounds—Esther was an orphan. But God has a habit of picking up nobodies and making them somebodies.

Overnight, God placed the orphan girl, Esther, in the palace. Her godly uncle, Mordecai, had raised her and groomed her for greatness. She knew she was special even if she didn't have pretty shoes and even if she lived in a little hut. Mordecai had taught her about her covenant relationship with God.

> God has a habit of picking up nobodies and making them somebodies.

Many times, like Esther, we are oblivious to God's plan for our lives. She probably dreamed of raising a traditional Jewish family, leading an ordinary life, not knowing she was meant for extraordinary things. I'm sure she dreamed of holding hands with her fiancé under the olive tree and planning her wedding ceremony. While she was planning everyday things, God was planning supernatural opportunities for her.

While we are so busy grabbing lesser things, ordinary things, mediocre things, God is planning extraordinary things for our future. Don't let anyone tell you that you can't reach for the stars. Even if you don't get there today, you possess the possibility that, maybe tomorrow, you will make it. *"We know that all things work together for good to those who love God, to those who are the called according to His purpose"* (Romans 8:28).

A godly man laid the groundwork in Esther's childhood to prepare her for her life assignment. When the king selected his new queen, out of all those women, he chose Esther.

Esther had been groomed, psychologically and spiritually, to become great. God often sets a mentor alongside to give insight, wisdom, and direction. Esther had her Mordecai, Ruth had her Naomi, and Mary had her Elizabeth. Timothy had the faith of his mother and grandmother. Paul wrote, *"I call to remembrance the genuine faith that is in you, which dwelt first in your grandmother Lois and your mother Eunice, and I am persuaded is in you also"* (2 Timothy 1:5).

You could be your children's mentor. What you speak into your children's lives today may prepare them for unexpected greatness and unlimited opportunities.

God had a higher purpose for young Esther than being the king's contest winner. Before this young girl was selected from her province to enter the contest, she didn't know proper protocol: she hadn't been taught formal table manners; she didn't know how to curtsy; she didn't know the right clothes to wear; she didn't display manners befitting royalty. Yet, God selected this ignorant orphan girl, fresh from the hills. Like Cinderella, her foot "fit the glass slipper," and she found favor with the king.

The king chose Esther, not because she was Jewish or because he had a spiritual revelation. He was simply using his senses, unaware that God was guiding his eyes.

Did you know that God is able to use people who aren't spiritual? Have you ever had someone say to you, "I don't know why I'm doing this for you; I don't know why I'm breaking the rules for you"? They're telling the truth—they don't know why they're helping you. They can't intelligently explain why they want to help you. God will even use your enemies to make a way for you when you're in His will. Proverbs 16:7 says, *"When a man's ways please the LORD, He makes even his enemies to be at peace with him."*

Once Esther was in the palace, she had to go through a purification process. Along with the call of God comes "the process." We like to be called out and chosen by God, but for every calling there is a discipline.

First, Esther had to soak in oil for six months. In Scripture, oil signifies the Holy Spirit. I'm sure her feet were calloused from walking barefoot in the hills and mountains. She had to be oiled down in order to smooth the skin between her toes and on the soles of her feet. Before God can use you, He has to soak you in the Holy Spirit to take away the rough places in your life.

> We like to be called by God, but for every calling there is discipline.

This woman was going to determine the fate of her nation. She had to be anointed. She was affecting future generations. Queen Vashti was an independent woman concerned with doing her own thing, but Esther understood it was not about her thing; it was about following God's plan.

By soaking in oil every day for six months, Esther represented a woman of God becoming extremely attuned to the Holy Spirit. Women, don't think you're a freak because you're spiritually sensitive. You're not a person who has only a mind and a body, but you also have a spirit. Therefore, you're spiritual, not just cute. You can wear a beautiful dress and makeup, but still have Holy Spirit anointing underneath. Don't be ashamed of your spirituality.

Men, sometimes your friends will make fun of you for being spiritually minded. They may mock your sensitivity and compassion while tempting you to revert back to your cold, detached, self-reliant past. Ask yourself, *How is that working out for my so-called "friends?"* Remember that it takes more courage and machismo to remain sensitive to the things of God than it does to run from Him and live life on your own.

The second step of Esther's purification process was being perfumed. You know what perfume does. It makes you smell nice; it draws people to you. In the Bible, incense represents our praise to God. There was an altar of incense in the Old Testament tabernacle. When the priest poured the perfume on the hot coals of the altar of incense, the scent would go up to heaven. The Bible says that God received the incense offering as a sweet-smelling savor of praise. (See Leviticus 2:2.) Of course, under the new covenant, we don't have to sprinkle incense on a fire. All we have to do is open up our mouths and give God the fruit of our lips, which is the fragrance of praise in His nostrils. (See Hebrews 13:15.)

When we praise God verbally, it's like spraying the most expensive perfume or cologne; it goes up to heaven and creates an aroma that gets God's attention. Praise is more than making a noise. When you praise Him, you invite the presence of God, the calm of God, and the serenity of God into your life.

Praise is called "the oil of myrrh." Remember the wise men who came to Bethlehem when Jesus was born? They brought frankincense and myrrh, which denote praise and adoration. Learn to be a worshipper.

Esther's scent reached the king before she did. The reason the king extended his scepter to Esther was that she filled the throne room with her perfume of praise before she was given access into the king's presence. We, too, come into God's presence first by the aroma of our praise.

No wonder the ultimate worshipper, the psalmist David, said, *"Enter into His gates with thanksgiving, and into His courts with praise. Be thankful to Him, and bless His name"* (Psalm 100:4). Esther was chosen, groomed, oiled, and perfumed.

When you praise, you get a sense of what God wants you to do. With praise comes prophecy. With praise comes direction. With praise comes God's plan for your life.

I'm sure that after six months of bubble baths, massages, pedicures, manicures, pampering, the opulence of the palace, and the luxurious lifestyle Esther was afforded, she began to dull a little spiritually. If you are not careful, you may become so pampered and comfortable spiritually that you will forget there is a godly reason for being where you are. This is no time to get comfortable! There is still a plot

> **With praise comes prophecy, direction, and God's plan for your life.**

to annihilate our children, our homes, our marriages, and our nation. You have a call of God upon your life; you have an appointment with destiny.

While Esther got comfortable and almost forgot her purpose, Mordecai put on sackcloth. (See Esther 4:1.) Sackcloth is ugly-looking clothing. He got ugly. Every now and then, we have to "get ugly" to get God's attention. We have to afflict ourselves with fasting and prayer.

Mordecai reminded Esther that she was not just there to look good and to wear beautiful clothing. No, there was a mission!

Do not think in your heart that you will escape in the king's palace any more than all the other Jews. For if you remain completely silent at this time, relief and deliverance will arise for the Jews from another place, but you and your father's house will perish. Yet who knows whether you have come to the kingdom for such a time as this? (Esther 4:13–14)

Don't forget your purpose. To all of you Esthers out there, there is a plot to destroy your family. We all enjoy being pampered, but there is a battle to fight and a victory to win. There is a cause!

Esther got the message from Mordecai, and she sent word back, saying, in effect, "I was a little foggy for a while. I went on a fantasy trip, but I'm back on course. I've made a decision about my purpose. I know what God has called me to do, and I've got to make this move." Esther said, *"And if I perish, I perish!"* (Esther 4:16). The result was that Esther preserved her race.

"Who knows whether you have come to the kingdom for such a time as this?" It is time for you to make your move. Up until now you've been merely looking the part. Gentlemen, you hang around in the back all cool and detached. Ladies, you sit in church like a fashion model. Now, your time is up. Maybe a couple of years ago you could afford to play God-games, but now it's your time. Don't forget your purpose. Move out and do it—submit to God's will. Be anointed with the oil of the Holy Spirit; be perfumed with passionate praise for God. You have come to the kingdom for such a time as this. Jesus prayed, *"Not My will, but Yours, be done"* (Luke 22:42). Pray and expect God to give you the right plan for your life.

Stay open to divine interruptions; when God does a new thing it's not like the old thing. Lot's wife only appears one time in the Old Testament. Why did Jesus tell us to remember her? (See Luke 17:32.) It was because she refused to break with her past. She turned into a lifeless monument. Stop rehearsing your beginning, and write the rest of your story. In Isaiah, God even told His prophet, *"Behold, I will do a new thing, now it shall spring forth"* (Isaiah 43:19). If you're afraid of the future, remember that He has never failed you.

Part III

Unlocking Discernment

Chapter Seven

WAIT ON THE LORD

Whoever believes will not act hastily.
—Isaiah 28:16

For a time in 2005, I was ashamed to tell anybody where I was from. Every time I turned on the news, all I saw and heard was "the Runaway Bride from Gainesville, Georgia." It was constant. My heart went out to those families, and to the bride herself, that such a personal and traumatic moment would suddenly become such public fodder.

The truth is, there are scores of bad marriages in this world because the people rushed into them. There was pressure or fear or emotion, and they just went ahead with it. People had told the Gainesville couple, "You need to wait." Counselors told them, "You need to wait." People they respected spiritually told them, "You need to wait." Let me weigh in with my two cents: if you are confused about whether or not you want to marry someone to the point that you're ready to run away, you don't need to marry that person—ever!

In 1 Samuel 13, we read about a man who had trouble waiting. Saul was the king of the nation of Israel, which was being besieged by the Philistine army. The prophet Samuel told Saul that war was indeed coming. Through Samuel, God instructed Saul to go to the temple and wait for seven days. After that, Samuel would come and offer a sacrifice, and God would then go with them into battle. Simple enough, right? Wrong.

Scripture says,

Then he waited seven days, according to the time set by Samuel. But Samuel did not come to Gilgal; and the people were scattered from him. So Saul said, "Bring a burnt offering and peace offerings here to me." And he offered the burnt offering. (1 Samuel 13:8–9)

Soon after that, Samuel arrived and Saul went out to greet him. Samuel asked what Saul had done. Saul replied,

When I saw that the people were scattered from me, and that you did not come within the days appointed, and that the Philistines gathered together at Michmash, then I said, "The Philistines will now come down on me at Gilgal, and I have not made supplication to the LORD." Therefore I felt compelled, and offered a burnt offering. (verses 11–12)

Do you hear what Saul was saying? "The people were expecting me to do something. You weren't here. Nothing was happening. I wasn't just going to sit there. I had to do something. The people expected me to do something."

Samuel's response was,

You have done foolishly. You have not kept the commandment of the LORD your God, which He commanded you. For now the LORD would have established your kingdom over Israel forever. But now your kingdom shall not continue.

The LORD has sought for Himself a man after His own heart, and the LORD has commanded him to be commander over His people, because you have not kept what the LORD commanded you. (1 Samuel 13:13–14)

Do you see what's going on here? If Saul had simply waited as he was instructed, there would have never been a need for David. The Lord would have established His kingdom with Saul.

God has a perfect time and a correct way for everything. We can get ourselves into trouble when we don't train ourselves to wait on Him. *"Whoever believes will not act hastily"* (Isaiah 28:16). If you believe that God only wants what is best for your life, and you are following Him, then He is ultimately in control of your life—your family, your career, your finances, your decisions, everything!

> We can get into trouble when we don't train ourselves to wait on the Lord.

In other words, don't rush into things! Don't do things because people are putting pressure on you. People can mess their lives up when they jump into things even though, in their hearts, they're hearing, *Hold on* and *Wait.*

"Whoever believes will not act hastily." Whoever believes will not quickly jump into anything.

But those who wait on the LORD shall renew their strength; they shall mount up with wings like eagles. (Isaiah 40:31)

Wait on the LORD; be of good courage, and He shall strengthen your heart; wait, I say, on the LORD!
(Psalm 27:14)

Waiting Financially

People today just have to have it all right now. Years ago, buying something on credit was actually considered a bad thing. It's what people with no money did. Now, people would never consider saving money for a big purchase. Why wait when you can have it now?

I've heard people say, "Well, I don't really feel a peace about that house, but we walked through it and we just felt chill bumps. It's the house we've always wanted." But can you afford that house? Can you make the payment every month?

Maybe now is not the right time. Does that mean that you can never have it? No, but it might mean that now is not the right time. Remember, *"whoever believes will not act hastily."*

People make stupid decisions trying to keep up with the Joneses, only to find out, when they catch up with the Joneses, that they are up to their eyeballs in debt. People make stupid financial decisions because they don't use discernment; they don't wait on the Lord. Wait and save your money. Be patient. Don't try to get everything now. Wait!

Don't Force It

God's timing is perfect. If you're being pressured, that's the time when you need to pull back. You need to pray and fast. You need to go to the Word. Then, after you've prayed with your spouse, fasted, and gone to the Word, you need to talk to some of your Christian friends, or perhaps a pastor, and say, "Help me pray about this." *"By the mouth of two or three witnesses"* (2 Corinthians 13:1) every major decision of your life ought to be confirmed. It should not just be you. You don't just walk through any opened door.

God does not push; God leads. God does not force; God leads. Don't jeopardize God's best by becoming impatient trying to make something happen in your life that only He can release. I think about how many men of God I've known who bit the dust because they became impatient. They began to think, *The rules don't apply to me anymore. I can take things into my own hands.* They climbed to incredible heights, reaching masses of people, but somewhere they lost touch with reality and raced ahead of God.

That is what happened to Saul. You have to be careful when God blesses you. You can get to the place where you believe that the rules, God's Word, don't apply to you anymore. Years earlier, God had spoken to Saul through the prophet Samuel, saying, "Saul, don't offer the sacrifice." But Saul's fear overcame his faith in God's Word, and he took matters into his own hands.

I don't care how much money you have. I don't care how much power you have. I don't care how much influence you have. I don't care what success you have. If you don't use discernment, if you don't wait on the Lord, it's only a matter of time before it catches up with you! You will become self-indulgent and lose your spiritual sensitivity. That's what happened to Saul.

If you are in the business world, you need to understand this. When God blesses you with prestige and position and power, you need spiritual discernment to know when you start to drift away and think the rules don't apply anymore. You need to continue to wait on the Lord and not resort to illegal or immoral shortcuts that fatten up the bottom line.

FACING YOUR GOLIATH

Here's why this is so important. While Saul was caught up in his own thing—offering his own sacrifices, not listening to anybody, not waiting on God—Goliath was on his way. Saul had never encountered Goliath before, but God knew Goliath was coming. Two chapters later, Goliath arrived to find Saul trembling in his tent. Why? When you begin to do your own thing, when you don't wait on the Lord or seek His counsel, Goliath shows up and you have no confidence—no courage. Saul was not ready to fight Goliath. Scripture says that by merely *"hearing the Philistine's words, Saul and all the Israelites were dismayed and terrified"* (1 Samuel 17:11). He was afraid because he hadn't learned to wait on the Lord. Fortunately, there was a boy named David who knew how to wait on the Lord, worship the Lord, and praise the Lord, so that, when Goliath came, he wasn't afraid.

I'm simply telling you this: Goliath is coming. You can't afford to disconnect from God. You can't afford to just ignore the convictions of the Holy Spirit and not wait on the Lord. Spend time with Him. Seek His face. Make no mistake, Goliath is coming. You say, "Oh, I've already faced it. Ooh. Let me tell my testimony." I promise you, another one will come! They come in seasons—the Goliath of something wrong with one of your children, the financial Goliath, the career Goliath, the health Goliath. I don't know what your Goliath will be, but I know it's coming and you don't want to be trembling in your tent when it does. You don't want to be cold and indifferent. You don't want to be ignoring everything God's told you to do when your Goliath comes.

> You don't want to be ignoring everything God told you when your Goliath comes.

Scripture states that Goliath was an overpowering figure, *"a man of war from his youth"* (1 Samuel 17:33). That means that many men had tried to defeat him in battle, but none ever had. When crisis comes, a fear will come in your heart. But if you are really in touch with God, something greater rises up inside of you and says, "I will not panic. I will not dread. I will not fear. God is with me. He's on the throne. It's going to be all right."

There are people reading this book who are going too fast and furious. They're trying to make something fit that doesn't fit. You're trying to force it to fit. Finally, you do kind of get it to fit, but now there's another piece that won't fit. It just messes the whole puzzle up. That's just like your life! If it doesn't fit, don't force it! If it doesn't feel right, wait on the Lord because *"whoever believes will not act hastily."*

Waiting on the Lord means that you will recognize His will and His voice. That doesn't mean that you become paralyzed by analyzing everything to death. It doesn't mean that you are waiting for an angel to appear, or putting out some kind of fleece.

Rest in the fact that God knows how to speak to His children and that *"by the mouth of two or three witnesses every word shall be established"* (2 Corinthians 13:1). Wait on Him and those witnesses will come forth. Even if it's a good opportunity, make sure it's a God opportunity!

Chapter Eight

GUARDING THE
UNGUARDED MOMENTS

*Blessed is the LORD God of Israel, who sent you this day
to meet me! And blessed is your advice and blessed are
you, because you have kept me this day from coming to
bloodshed and from avenging myself with my own hand.*

—1 Samuel 25:32–33

It's a typical Sunday morning in the Franklin home. I'm
up and out at 5:00 a.m., putting the finishing touches
on my sermon. Back at the house, Cherise is left to deal
with getting five kids dressed and ready for church. Have you
ever tried to get five kids ready for church by yourself, plus get
yourself ready? Sometimes she feels like she's in a trial run for
the battle of Armageddon!

One Sunday morning, I received a frantic phone call. "I've
had it," she said. "I can't take it anymore. I've reached my
breaking point." After she had all the kids fully dressed, Drake,
our seven-year-old, spilled something all over his clothes.
Connar, our eight-year-old, could not find her shoes anywhere.

Courteney and Caressa, our teenagers, were fighting over who got to wear what blouse. Caroline, our twelve-year-old, had eaten too much candy the night before and was feeling sick.

There's nothing like the joy of getting ready to be in the house of the Lord! By the time Cherise arrived at church, twenty minutes late, she was so frazzled she wished she had pulled the sheets over her head and stayed in bed!

THE "UNGUARDED MOMENT"

Have you ever been there? If so, you know how David felt when he had what I call an "unguarded moment."

David was anointed king during Saul's reign over Israel. But he did not go to the throne immediately. He was anointed at seventeen, but he was not appointed until he was about thirty.

As David's thirtieth birthday approached, the clock was ticking and none of God's promises had come to fruition in his life. How can God say one thing, but the circumstances of your life say otherwise? Often, before you reach your dream, you will experience the opposite of what you want. Abraham was dreaming for Isaac, the promised child; but first he experienced Ishmael, the problem child. The children of Israel were dreaming for a land flowing with milk and honey, but first they experienced the desert with no food or water. Jacob dreamed of a beautiful bride named Rachel, but first he was tricked into marrying Leah.

To make matters worse, David was leading six hundred men who were in debt, under distress, and feeling discontented. David rose to the task of training them into a mighty army.

One day, they approached the vineyard of a man named Nabal, a rich man married to a very beautiful and intelligent woman named Abigail. Although Nabal acted foolishly, Abigail used her discernment to honor David, the man of God. (See 1 Samuel 25:2–42.) David's men decided to protect and guard Nabal's vineyard, and instead of asking for payment in money, they asked for food to replenish their strength. Nabal acted just like his name, which means "foolish." He refused to give them any food, and then, adding insult to injury, he accused David of being a servant who had broken away from his master. In other words, he called David a "nobody." Nabal insulted David by refusing him.

In order to appreciate David's reaction, you need to understand the crucial point at which David was living at that moment. David represents men who are in a transition in their lives; men who are close to reaching their dreams, yet whose fulfillment seems so far away. They're living on an unrealized promise! David had to be wondering, *Did God really say that I would reign as king, or was I just fantasizing?*

For thirteen years, David had been hanging on to that promise. He had believed God every step of the way, but now he had come to his breaking point. At this tender, touchy moment, along came Nabal. In the midst of David's spiritual frustration, what God had said about his future was not foremost in his mind. All he could think about at that moment was his location and his hunger.

In this unguarded moment, David assembled four hundred of his fiercest warriors and said, *"Every man gird on his sword"* (1 Samuel 25:13). And they set out to kill Nabal and his entire family.

Nabal was about to feel David's wrath. With his promised

goals and throne eluding him, David lost it. How many of us can relate to this? Endless loads of thankless laundry, screaming children, unsympathetic bosses, then somebody cuts you off in traffic and you just want to scream, "I can't take it anymore!" You've reached the breaking point! You're having an unguarded moment.

You never know when it's going to happen. Human emotion is unpredictable. And Christians are certainly not exempt from those times when life's pressure brings out our rawest, deepest emotions. Yet, all it takes is that one unguarded moment and you can lose your reputation, your testimony, and even your ministry.

> One unguarded moment can lose your reputation, testimony, and ministry.

One Wednesday night some time ago, I experienced an unguarded moment. I was taking the children home from our Wednesday night service. Cherise had gone out of town, and I had all five of the children by myself. I finally had them all hooked into their car seats and started on our way home when they informed me that they were starving.

We stopped at a fast-food restaurant down the road that has big yellow arches! The Wednesday night prior, we had stopped at the same restaurant and gone through the drive-thru window where I specifically asked for five cheeseburger kids' meals with no onions and no pickles. We drove all the way home, and, when the children opened up their food, onions were all over the place. They all threw fits and went to bed hungry, and I felt frustrated.

So, here we were again the following Wednesday night, same restaurant, same drive-thru, same lady at the window. I rolled down my window and began to speak to the little box. I was extremely nice, of course, because I'm Pastor Franklin—and because some of my members were in the line behind me!

I pleaded with the little box, "Please, ma'am, no onions. This is extremely important: no onions and no pickles. We asked for this last week, and you didn't do it. Please take care of it this week. Make sure our cheeseburgers have no onions and no pickles."

She said, "I'll handle it."

We pulled on through and were handed our five meals. The kids asked, "Can we eat it in the car, Dad?" "Absolutely not," I responded, "you are going to eat it at home. I'm not going to have that mess in my car for another month!"

We made it home, and I walked in the door with two or three of the kids screaming like they were starving to death. I opened up cheeseburger number one and looked at it—no onions, and no pickles...and no meat! There was only a slice of cheese with a blob of ketchup and mustard! I took cheeseburger number two, ditto! I looked at cheeseburger number three, same thing! By now, steam was whistling out of my ears and my eyes were rolling around in my head like the child in *The Exorcist*. I was ready to tell somebody what they could do with those cheeseburgers!

I called the restaurant and demanded, "I want a manager! Who owns this restaurant? I want a name and a phone number!" The girls were very supportive, saying, "Get 'em, Daddy! Get 'em, Daddy! You tell 'em, Daddy!" About halfway through, it dawned on me that I had just stood in the pulpit that evening, and now I was about to let somebody have it. Perhaps I wasn't going to kill somebody, like David, but wasn't it

Jesus who said, *"You have heard that it was said...'Do not murder, and anyone who murders will be subject to judgment.' But I tell you that anyone who is angry with his brother will be subject to judgment"* (Matthew 5:21–22 NIV)? Oops.

In David's life, at the point when he was about to kill Nabal, God sent a woman of great discernment into his life. It's always good to have discerning people around you. Abigail's wisdom had nothing to do with her beauty, her education, or the fact that she was married to a wealthy man. She had discernment because she feared the Lord, and she could think fast to defuse an explosive situation in her home. She believed what God had said about David—that he truly would become king—so she stood firmly on the Word of God to save her family. In this critical, transitional time in David's life, he needed to run into an Abigail.

It's always good for us to meet an Abigail, but especially when we're in transition. When we're trying to build a small business, but can't get the loan. When we're counting on getting a raise, but it hasn't come through yet. When we're searching for a job, but haven't found one. When we've got to relocate, but can't sell the old house. When we're chasing our dream, but can't quite reach the top. These are dangerous, tricky times, times when we need an Abigail to cross our path.

When Abigail heard that David was coming to destroy her family, she did not crumble in the face of impending crisis. Instead, she prepared baskets of food. She knew from God's Word, *"A soft answer turns away wrath, but a harsh word stirs up anger"* (Proverbs 15:1). She carefully picked her timing, and went to meet David. When she arrived, she met him with a meal. She fed him, calmed him down, and got him to relax.

Ladies, how do you deal with the temper of a man who is going through a transition? A man who seems so far from his vision, one who is frustrated, broken, and seems to have lost his dream? How do you deal with a man when he doesn't have enough money? The answer is not the divorce court, nor packing your bags and going to your mother's house. You need to ask God to give you discernment and a wise tongue. Being a true woman of God is being able to speak with a wise tongue to a man in transition. You can be his dream restorer.

The first thing Abigail did when she met David was to honor him. Believe me, he didn't look like anything worth honoring. Here was a man who lived in a cave with six hundred rejects. He didn't have any possessions to his name; all he had was a promise from God. But she showed honor to that dirty, smelly, angry, unreasonable man.

And it shall come to pass, when the LORD *has done for my lord according to all the good that He has spoken concerning you, and has appointed you ruler over Israel.*

(1 Samuel 25:30)

In referring to him as *"lord,"* she acknowledged that she was in the presence of a king. David did not look like a king. He wasn't wearing a crown on his head, but Abigail said, in effect, "I believe what God says about you." She was using the word of God to save her family and her future. She kept on using the word, and it got inside David. It took away his temper. It took away his violence. It took away his anger.

Many times, we just don't want to use the promise God has given us—His Word. We would rather use our intellect and wit. We would rather use manipulation and control. That is why many marriages are unhappy—there is no love in the home.

I dare you to ask God what He thinks about the person you are sleeping next to. Ask God what He says about your spouse. We give up too soon! You can either be a person of faith like Abigail, or a fool like Job's wife, who advised her husband to curse God and die. (See Job 2:9.)

God's Word is incapable of lying. So, keep talking about it until the Word becomes flesh. Remember to talk to the king in your man, and the king will stand up. Call out the queen in your wife, and the queen will emerge. David said, *"Blessed is the Lord God of Israel, who sent you this day to meet me! And blessed is your advice and blessed are you, because you have kept me this day from coming to bloodshed and from avenging myself with my own hand"* (1 Samuel 25:32–33).

There will be times in your life when you will feel like giving up on the dream God has given you. Before you destroy your destiny by doing something you will regret, God will always send the Holy Spirit, as He sent Abigail, to intercept you and remind you of what God has said about your future. *"For I know the thoughts that I think toward you, says the Lord, thoughts of peace and not of evil, to give you a future and a hope"* (Jeremiah 29:11).

BEING THE VOICE OF DISCERNMENT FOR OTHERS

Is there anyone in your life who is in transition? Like David, are they in that in-between place where they just can't seem to get where they are trying to go? Ask God to give you discernment and a wise tongue. You could be the voice of discernment, speaking the Word of God into their "unguarded moment," stopping them from throwing away their destiny. Anybody can believe in him- or herself when they are on top of the world, but those with the gift of discernment will speak out in the valley, calling things that are not as though they were. The discerning believer sees potential in people when they don't see it. Pray for God to give you the right words to speak to those in transition, to help restore their dreams.

Nabal died a premature death three weeks later. David went on to become a great king. David eventually married Abigail. In saving David's future, Abigail also secured her own.

As I think back on my ministry, my mind races through many years to two or three critical moments when leaving seemed easier than staying. During one particularly hard time, I was greatly discouraged. Division was wreaking havoc in our church. Some people left, people whom I thought would never leave. It seemed the problems just kept on coming, one after another after another. Everything I had worked for felt like it was hanging by a thread. It was the darkest hour of my pastorate.

> The discerning believer sees potential in people when they don't see it.

To make matters worse, while driving home one day, I rear-ended a car at a stop sign. Even though it was just a fender bender, it felt like I couldn't do anything right. When I walked in the door of my home, the phone rang. It was the person whom I had rear-ended. His first question was, "Are you that guy who pastors that big church?" He informed me that, all of a sudden, his neck and back were hurting. A lawsuit seemed imminent. At that moment, something inside of me collapsed.

After dealing with the church problems for months, the straw that broke the camel's back broke mine, and I began to weep. I consider myself to be a strong, "can-do" person. I am not a quitter. But, at that moment, I had reached the end of my strength.

I will never forget how my wife instantly discerned my vulnerability. At that critical moment, she took control of the situation. She immediately got on the phone and dealt with the crisis, defusing it masterfully. She spoke confidently to me about my future. By the time she got through with me, I felt like I could whip a pack of lions.

How strange. I had always been the person giving hope and encouragement to others with my preaching. But this time, God wanted to encourage me.

I know without a doubt, had I not felt my wife's strength at that moment, had she not stood up to the crisis and become the discerning voice of God to me about my future, I would have left the ministry in defeat.

> Never underestimate the power God has placed in you to discern for loved ones.

Never underestimate the power God has placed in you to discern the seasons your loved ones are experiencing. Don't drown out that voice on the inside, for it could be the voice that restores their dreams.

Now, years later, thousands of people attend Free Chapel. We have a one-hundred-fifty-acre campus, a beautiful new sanctuary, and outreach programs that win thousands of souls. But it all teetered that afternoon on the discernment of my wife. When I reflect on the discernment and strength Cherise exhibited that day in my unguarded moment, I feel like David when he said to Abigail, in effect, "Blessed is the God of Israel, who sent you to me to keep me from sinning." (See 1 Samuel 25:33.)

The Holy Spirit will speak to you when your family needs encouragement. Your tongue can make or break your loved ones. The impressions the Holy Spirit gives you about them are for a reason. Pray, and wait for the right time in their lives when God will open the door for you to speak to them. Discernment will let you know when to back off and give them some space, and when to speak up with the truth that has been revealed to you.

If my wife had put me down that day during my unguarded moment, I dare not think where my family or ministry would be today. I thank God that I had an Abigail in my life; I had a voice of discernment.

Chapter Nine

UNLOCKING DISCERNMENT WITH PRAYER

I will give you the keys of the kingdom of heaven.
—Matthew 16:19

Here is a precious secret I've learned: prayer invites angels into the war zone of your experience.

In Acts, King Herod imprisoned the apostle Peter, guarding him with four squads of soldiers. They were no match, however, for the prayers of the believers. *"Peter was therefore kept in prison, but constant prayer was offered to God for him by the church"* (Acts 12:5). And the result?

> *That night Peter was sleeping, bound with two chains between two soldiers; and the guards before the door were keeping the prison. Now behold, an angel of the Lord stood by him, and a light shone in the prison; and he struck Peter on the side and raised him up, saying, "Arise quickly!" And his chains fell off his hands.* (verses 6–7)

When you pray, God dispatches angels.

Jesus prayed in the garden of Gethsemane, and angels came and ministered to Him. (See Luke 22:43.)

Paul prayed in the midst of a storm, out in the middle of an ocean, and God sent an angel to stand by him. (See Acts 27:23.)

When you pray, God releases angels. No matter what you're going through, they stand by you. If this is true, then one of the greatest tragedies of prayerlessness is the scores of unemployed angels just waiting to be dispatched by God. Angels are attracted to the place of prayer.

Charles Haddon Spurgeon pastored the first mega-church of ten thousand members in London, England, back in the 1800s. His sermons were published and still inspire millions today. Although you've probably heard of Charles Spurgeon, I doubt very much that you've ever heard of James Spurgeon. James was Charles's brother and business manager.

> The greatest people on earth are those who pray.

When Charles Spurgeon took the pulpit at Metropolitan Tabernacle, James went under the pulpit, into a secret prayer closet. The key to Charles Spurgeon's powerful preaching was his brother's powerful praying. Prayer builds a power base, allowing you to do what God commands you to do. We've seen the power of disagreement destroy churches and homes; it's time to see the power of agreement in prayer ignite our churches and homes, as well as revive us personally.

The greatest people on earth are people who pray. I don't mean people who talk about prayer, nor people who believe in prayer, nor even those who can explain prayer beautifully;

I mean people who put in the time on their knees in prayer. These folks aren't necessarily blessed with spare hours to pray—they make the time by taking time away from less important things. Put prayer first and your schedule second. The prevailing prayer of faith is the power on earth that employs the power of heaven. Whatever you do after that is merely gathering up the results of prayer.

Prayer has brought hearing to the deaf, sight to the blind, life to the dead, salvation to the lost, and healing to the sick. Prevailing prayer should be the main business of our day.

Every day, we must pray!

If prayer is anything, prayer is everything. If the church will not pray, God will not act. For Jesus said, *"I will give you the keys of the kingdom of heaven"* (Matthew 16:19).

PREVAILING PRAYER

What is prevailing prayer? It is not foxhole praying—praying only when you are in a crisis. It is not halfhearted, lukewarm, lay-me-down-to-sleep prayer. Prevailing prayer is wrestling against principalities and powers. Paul said, *"Therefore I exhort first of all that supplications, prayers, intercessions, and giving of thanks be made for all men"* (1 Timothy 2:1). It is the protracted prayer, fasting prayer, weeping prayer, effectual prayer, and fervent prayer of the righteous that avails much. (See James 5:16.)

The power of prevailing prayer is evident in James's account of the prophet Elijah influencing the weather with his prayers. *"Elijah was a man with a nature like ours, and he prayed earnestly that it would not rain; and it did not rain on the land for three years and six months. And he prayed again, and the heaven gave rain, and the earth produced its fruit"* (James 5:17–18). (See also 1 Kings 17.)

113

Prevailing prayer is Esther fasting for three days and saving her nation by causing the enemies of the Jews to be defeated. (See Esther 4:16.) That's prevailing prayer!

Prevailing prayer is Hagar interceding before the Lord, *"Let me not see the death of the boy* [Ishmael]*"* (Genesis 21:16). God heard her prayer and blessed Ishmael because of the prevailing prayer of a mother.

Prevailing prayer is Rizpah, a concubine who bore two sons with King Saul. David gave the two boys to the Gibeonites to atone for Saul's treatment of them. The two boys were subsequently hung by the neck until they died. Afterward, the boys' remains were not cut down, but remained to be devoured by wild beasts. Rizpah, their mother, would not be satisfied with that. So, she took a piece of sackcloth and spread it upon a rock. For five months, she sat there in a vigil with nothing left but the bones of her boys. She used to adorn herself with silk in the king's court, but now, after months of sitting on a rock fighting for what was left of her family, I'm sure she was wild-eyed and haggard, like a lioness guarding her cubs. She didn't forsake them through the wind, rain, cold, or sun, not even through the attacks of the wild beasts and vultures. She would not give up on her children until they were cut down and let loose. (See 2 Samuel 21:10–14.)

Finally, word reached King David about what she was doing. He gave a command to bury the boys with Saul in graves belonging to kings. Scripture tells us that, *"They performed all that the king commanded. And after that God heeded the prayer for the land"* (verse 14). Because Rizpah prevailed, a king was moved, her sons were honored with burials in the tomb of kings, and God heard their prayers.

Prevailing prayer is having the tenacity to hold on until something happens. One of the greatest weaknesses of this generation is a lack of commitment for the long haul. The fastest animal on earth is the African cheetah. It has been measured at seventy miles per hour. However, the cheetah has one problem: it has a small heart, so it tires quickly. If it doesn't catch its prey quickly, it won't last. Some people have a cheetah approach to prayer. They lack heart to sustain the effort for the long haul. They burst out in prayer, but it doesn't last long. Why have a cheetah heart when God wants you to have an eagle heart? Isaiah 40:31 says,

> **Prevailing prayer is having the tenacity to hold on until something happens.**

"Those who wait on the LORD shall renew their strength; they shall mount up with wings like eagles, they shall run and not be weary."

THE POWER OF EFFECTIVE PRAYER

Why is it that Christians often neglect prayer? I believe we do not understand the effect our prayers have in the spirit realm. As I was reading Revelation one day, some verses seemed to leap off the page:

> *Golden bowls full of incense, which are the prayers of the saints.* (Revelation 5:8)

> *The smoke of the incense, with the prayers of the saints, ascended before God....Then the angel took the censer, filled it with fire from the altar, and threw it to the earth.* (Revelation 8:4–5)

What marvelous images! When you pray, you are filling the prayer bowls of heaven. In God's perfect timing, your prayers are mixed with the fire of God (His power) and cast back down to earth to change your situation. Your prayers don't just bounce off the ceiling; they rise like incense before the throne of God!

Even if you don't feel like anything is happening in the natural world, when you pray, you are filling the prayer bowls in the spirit realm. When they are full, they will tilt and pour out answers to your prayers!

A GENERATION IN PERIL

I believe that God is ready to tilt the prayer bowl on this generation. Today, one out of three babies are aborted in this nation. Why is the devil trying to keep this generation from being born? I believe it is because God has something special in mind for this generation, and the devil knows it. The first generation Satan tried to keep from being born was Moses' generation. Pharaoh decreed that all the male children under the age of two were to be killed. Moses' generation was a deliverance generation.

The second generation Satan tried to eliminate was Jesus' generation. King Herod decreed that all the children, again under the age of two, were to be killed. This was another deliverance generation.

Now, Satan has staked his claim to a third generation—your generation. The reason there is such an attack on this generation through abortion is that you are destined to be a deliverance generation! No matter what kind of hell you're going through, you must prevail in prayer until you tilt the bowl in heaven.

Some time ago, I read the true story of a pilot in a small plane who noticed a warning light indicating an open door on the plane. He got up to check it out and, just as he got there, the door blew open and sucked him out of the plane.

The copilot radioed back to the tower, "I'm coming back. The pilot just got sucked out of the plane! Send rescue choppers to search for his body." What the copilot didn't know was, when the door flew open and pulled the pilot out, the emergency ladder fell—and clinging to it for dear life was the pilot.

In fifteen minutes, the copilot landed the plane, unaware that the pilot's head was only three inches from the concrete. When onlookers realized what was happening, they ran out onto the airstrip to help the pilot. They had to pry his fingers loose one finger at a time.

> Prayer and discernment go hand in hand.

Do you know what you call that? Perseverance! Hanging in there! Prevailing prayer is hanging in there until you fill the prayer bowls.

Prayer and discernment go hand in hand. God is in need of men and women who will stand in the gap and become prevailing prayer warriors. In 1 Timothy, Paul pleaded with the church, *"I desire therefore that the men pray everywhere, lifting up holy hands, without wrath and doubting"* (1 Timothy 2:8). In Acts, Paul had a vision in which a man was saying, "Come to Macedonia." When Paul arrived there, he didn't find a man but, instead, found a group of women praying by the river. (See Acts 16:13.) Because of these women's prayers in Macedonia, Paul changed his direction. If those women had not been praying, Paul would not have gone west but east toward Asia.

Prayer, discernment, and service are the foundations on which the church is built. Prayer has been at the forefront of every major revival that has taken place on this earth.

PRAYER: AN INSATIABLE HUNGER FOR CHANGE

Proverbs 30:15–16 says,

The horseleach hath two daughters, crying, Give, give. There are three things that are never satisfied, yea, four things say not, It is enough. The grave; and the barren womb; the earth that is not filled with water; and the fire that saith not, It is enough.   (KJV)

Horseleach is a strange word and is only used once in the entire Bible. It is a bloodsucker, a greedy thing that has an awesome appetite. It just can't get enough. This text says the horseleach has two daughters who cry, *"Give, give."* The double annunciation is important. This Scripture is saying there are four things that are never satisfied:

1. The grave

If you visit Arlington National Cemetery in Washington, D.C., you will see white crosses as far as the eye can see. Thousands and thousands of soldiers have passed away, and yet the grave is still hungry. It still reaches up with grassy teeth, grabs men by the ankles, and pulls them down. The grave never gets enough. It doesn't respect old or young, male or female. It just keeps crying, "Give, give!"

2. The earth that is not filled with water

The ocean is fed by mighty rivers such as the Mississippi, the Niagara, the Nile, and the Amazon. Yet, with all the water flowing in from all over the world, the oceans never cover the earth. Water falls from the sky and rises up from the ground. Floods and rivers explode their banks, but the ocean gets filled with water. It just keeps crying and crying, "Give, give!"

3. Fire

Think of the great fires of history: The Great Chicago Fire, the San Francisco Fire of 1906, or the Great Fire of London. Fire swallows up businesses, hotels, and homes. Yet, it never becomes full. The more you put in its way, the more it takes. It's a horseleach. It keeps crying, "Give, give!"

4. The barren womb

How can the writer of Proverbs compare the barren womb to a fire that is never satisfied, to the ocean that is never full, or to the grave that never has enough? What is God saying? The great lesson contained in here is this: God is not moved by gentle suggestion, nor is He moved by passive people.

> The miraculous works of God were the result of insatiable hunger for change.

God is not shaken because we mumble a quick, little prayer. In the history of the Bible, all of the miraculous works of God were the result of incessant, enormous, insatiable hunger for change.

As thirsty as the ocean is to swallow up rivers and not be quenched, as hungry as fire is to eat up everything it can get and still look for fuel, as unsatisfied as the grave is to take in millions yet still cry daily for more, as insistent as a barren woman is that God give her children or she will die—that's how much we must desire to see the promises of God fulfilled. How do we birth God's will in the earth? We travail in prayer. The word *travail* expresses the pain and hard work of birthing a baby. No man knows about that word on the same level as a woman. Perhaps that's why women are so powerful in prayer.

As the ocean desires water, as fire consumes fuel, as the grave hungers for bones, so must the people of God crave a movement of God that bears souls and revival. When God gets ready to birth a promise, He looks for the barren soul who will cry, "Give, give!" He looks for sons and daughters of the horse-leach!

In Genesis, Rachel was the true love of Jacob. Unfortunately, Rachel was barren and had to stand by and watch as Jacob fathered children by his other wives. Finally, the hunger of this barren woman could take no more as she pleaded with Jacob and with God, *"Give me children, or else I die!"* (Genesis 30:1). Eventually, after much travailing, *"God remembered Rachel, and God listened to her and opened her womb"* (verse 22). She gave birth to Joseph. Years later, Rachel bore a second son, Benjamin.

To whom will revival be given? It will come to people who are as hungry as a grave, as thirsty as a river, and as ravenous as a fire. It comes to the congregation who never stops crying, "Give, give!" Prevailing prayer is Rachel praying, *"Give me children, or else I die!"* Oh, how we need men and women of prayer in the church again!

In the early days of the Christian church, the explosion of believers was threatening to bring it down. In the natural, they just couldn't meet all the needs of the hurting. So the disciples called a meeting,

The twelve summoned the multitude of the disciples and said, "It is not desirable that we should leave the word of God and serve tables. Therefore, brethren, seek out from among you seven men of good reputation, full of the Holy

Spirit and wisdom, whom we may appoint over this business; but we will give ourselves continually to prayer and to the ministry of the word."　　　　　　(Acts 6:2–4)

The apostles were torn between the work of the ministry and time spent in prayer. But they also knew that if they didn't give up on prayer, they wouldn't have to choose between the two—they could have both. They knew that ministry without prayer was powerless and ineffective. But it would take more than just the occasional prayer. They knew the stakes. They knew that they needed to devote themselves *"continually to prayer."*

In Luke 18, we see the power of persistent prayer. Sometimes you just have to keep asking. In Jesus' parable, a widow appeared before a judge repeatedly, but her request fell on deaf ears. She didn't get discouraged; she didn't quit. You must be persistent. Finally, the woman persisted so long, the judge said, in effect, "I don't usually do this, and under normal circumstances I wouldn't. But I've got to do something for this woman or she's going to wear me out." (See Luke 18:1–5.) You have to become "a spiritual pest." Every time God looks up, let Him see you before Him.

> The apostles knew that ministry without prayer was powerless.

You have to desire it so much that you tell God, "I'm going to wear You out. I'm going to keep praying until You save my children, until You bless my family. I'm going to remain before You. Jesus, I'm going to be a spiritual pest and wear You out. I'm not going to break down; I'm about to have a breakthrough."

Not long ago, a friend of mine named Tommy Tenney, author of *The God Chasers,* introduced me to a great woman of God. She has a reputation as a true prayer warrior. She and her husband started a church in Alexandria, Louisiana, where they established a prayer meeting that has never stopped. For over thirty years, twenty-four hours a day, there has been someone in that church praying.

Her son is now the pastor of this great church where thousands attend. Early on, she made God a promise concerning her son. She vowed to God that she would fast and pray on his birthday all the days of his life, from sunup to sundown. For over fifty years, on her son's birthday, she has gone to the church in the early hours of the day to shut herself away and pray all day for her son without food. As a result, he has become a great man of God.

When former President Bill Clinton first met her son, he was still the governor of Arkansas. He was so impressed with this minister that, even after becoming president, he would often fly into town just to attend his church for special services. Clinton invited her son to the White House several times to minister to him, especially during turbulent times.

For over fifty years, that silver-haired mother has prayed and fasted all day for her son on his birthday. Her persistence moved her son from the small, obscure town of Alexandria, Louisiana, all the way to the most powerful office in the world.

God is not looking for ability; He is looking for availability. You are part of an army that God is raising up to crush the enemy's skull. I have heard God say, "Get My people praying again. I'm going to use them in the final battle."

Chapter Ten

Discerning Women
Always Make a Difference

The Lord gave the word; great was the company
of those [women, NASB] who proclaimed it.
—Psalm 68:11

O ne of Satan's greatest fears is that women will find out who they really are and what a significant role they play in his ultimate downfall. The truth is, Satan is afraid of women because they are God's secret weapons for the final battle.

Why would God use women? I believe the answer is simple: the opening round of the battle was between the devil and a woman (Eve). Consequently, it is logical that the last round of this important final thrust should also include women.

The verse above depicts an army on the march, proclaiming the gospel. The biblical record shows that women have not been relegated to mere privates in God's army; they have been chosen as key players to transform the world. How fascinating it is that, even in the male-dominated Jewish culture, God made it a priority to include several discerning women as key figures in history.

DISCERNING WOMEN OF SCRIPTURE: DEBORAH

In Judges, the men of Israel hesitated when they received directions from God. Deborah, a prophetess, discerned God's instruction and decided to make a difference:

Then she [Deborah] *sent and called for Barak the son of Abinoam from Kedesh in Naphtali, and said to him, "Has not the LORD God of Israel commanded, 'Go and deploy troops at Mount Tabor; take with you ten thousand men of the sons of Naphtali and of the sons of Zebulun; and against you I will deploy Sisera, the commander of Jabin's army, with his chariots and his multitude at the River Kishon; and I will deliver him into your hand'?" And Barak said to her, "If you will go with me, then I will go; but if you will not go with me, I will not go!" So she said, "I will surely go with you; nevertheless there will be no glory for you in the journey you are taking, for the LORD will sell Sisera into the hand of a woman." Then Deborah arose and went with Barak to Kedesh.*

(Judges 4:6–9)

Two major things opposed Deborah that day. First, she was a woman in a male-dominated society. Second, she didn't have a sword with which to fight. But when Deborah got involved, God brought the army to her.

If you will decide to make a difference, then God will make *up* the difference. You have to believe in yourself, if only because God believes in you. You may feel inadequate to complete the task, but that's all right. Remember, God's supernatural involvement requires faith.

Deborah arose to lead God's people to victory over Sisera, the evil captain of the Canaanite army, who was reduced to running for his life. He ducked into a woman's tent to hide, thinking an ordinary housewife wasn't much of a threat to him. But while he was sleeping, this ordinary woman named Jael took a tent peg and drove it through his temple, killing him. (See Judges 4:17–21.) Think of what a surprise it must have been to hear the news that Sisera, the mighty warrior, had been slain by a housewife with a tent peg.

You can make a difference. God wants to raise up an army of housewives to proclaim His good news and defeat all His enemies that are coming against the family and the church.

In Genesis 33, when Jacob had to face his brother, Esau, after stealing the blessing, he was afraid for his life. Esau and four hundred of his soldiers were approaching with fire in their eyes. Do you know what Jacob did? He put all the women out in front and hid behind them. When Esau saw the women, he broke down and began to weep. (See Genesis 33:1–7.) The presence of women on the front line altered the spirit of the enemy.

Or, consider the New Testament account of the resurrection:

Now when the Sabbath was past, Mary Magdalene, Mary the mother of James, and Salome bought spices, that they might come and anoint Him. Very early in the morning, on the first day of the week, they came to the tomb when the sun had risen....Now when He rose early on the first day of the week, He appeared first to Mary Magdalene, out of whom He had cast seven demons. She went and told those who had been with Him, as they mourned and wept. And when they heard that He was alive and had been seen by her, they did not believe. (Mark 16:1–2, 9–11)

Here was the greatest single moment in the history of the world, and the only witness was a woman. This, to me, is ironclad proof that Scripture comes from God and not from men. In the Jewish culture, women had few rights. They couldn't teach or even become educated. Because of this, they were not allowed to testify in legal matters. Their voice meant nothing. If it were left to Jewish men to invent the Scriptures, they would have never left a woman to be the only witness of Jesus' resurrection. But God knew that only a discerning woman would be able to see and believe that, contrary to apparent circumstances, Jesus is alive!

> Scripture's message is there is weakness in strength and strength in weakness.

WHO? ME?

Don't be ashamed if, when God calls your number, your first response is, "Who? Me?" If you've never said those words, then I suspect that God has never talked to you. Whenever we respond to God, saying, "I'm not able to do that," God responds back, "Well, good. Now that we've got that out of the way, are you ready?"

God is never drawn to full; He is only drawn to empty. In fact, more believers fail because of their strengths than because of weaknesses. The ironic message of Scripture is that there is weakness in strength and strength in weakness. (See 2 Corinthians 12:9–10.)

The weakness of strength is found in the story of King Uzziah. He was sixteen when he began to reign. As long as he sought the Lord, God caused him to prosper. His fame spread far and wide. Then we come to a haunting phrase: *"But when he was strong his heart was lifted up, to his destruction"* (2 Chronicles 26:16). A mistaken notion in Christianity is that God is looking for strong people. Wrong! God is looking for weak people whose strength comes from Him.

The strength of weakness always begins with brokenness. Paul was stoned and left for dead, an oozing mass of broken bones. He was broken internally. He was hurting emotionally, mentally, and physically. Paul was a broken man, but oh, the strength of weakness! When properly responded to, weakness always leads to graduated blessing. God's answer to Paul was, *"My grace is sufficient for you, for My strength is made perfect in weakness"* (2 Corinthians 12:9).

When is God's grace sufficient to help you? When you look around and there is nothing left but the grace of God. As long as something else remains, we will tend to place our trust in it.

Paul's response to God was, *"Most gladly I will rather boast in my infirmities, that the power of Christ may rest upon me"* (verse 9). Stop looking at your weakness and begin to concentrate on His strength.

God's Army of Broken Women

God is mobilizing and equipping a female army to build His church and do His work in these last days. Spiritual leaders and ministries across the country are rising up to host women's conferences. Bishop T. D. Jakes started teaching "Woman, Thou Art Loosed" in a Sunday school class. Later, it became a best-selling book and hit movie. Today, his Woman Thou Art Loosed Conferences attract over fifty thousand women annually.

You might be surprised to learn what kind of women God is going to use in this end-time army. Only four women are mentioned in the genealogy of Jesus Christ. They are four of the "bad girls" of the Old Testament—Rahab was a harlot, Ruth was a former pagan and outcast widow with no right to marry an Israelite, Bathsheba was an adulteress, and Tamar was the widow who seduced her father-in-law. (See Matthew 1:3, 5–6.) It sure would seem that God could have found better women to make up the family tree of Jesus Christ!

I believe God deliberately chose these four women because He was trying to teach us about the power of redemption. After all, if women with that kind of past could be part of the physical family of Jesus Christ, then maybe the spiritual family of Christ, which is the church, can also include women with sordid pasts, now washed and cleansed by the blood of Jesus Christ.

> **If He brought you this far, God can get you from where you are to where you ought to be.**

You may not be all you ought to be, but, thank God, you're not what you used to be. If God could get you from where you were to where you are, then He can take you from where you are to where you ought to be! Don't let your past haunt you. Paul, who had a murderous history himself, told us, *"One thing I do, forgetting those things which are behind and reaching forward to those things which are ahead"* (Philippians 3:13). No matter your past, you can still reach for the future. God said through Isaiah, *"Do not remember the former things, nor consider the things of old. Behold, I will do a new thing, now it shall spring forth; shall you not know it? I will even make a road in the wilderness and rivers in the desert"* (Isaiah 43:18–19).

BREAKING FREE FROM YOUR SELF

You really can make a difference. But to become a discerning woman in God's army, you need to break free from the bondage of self-pity, self-loathing, and low self-esteem. Many things that happen to us in life can bind us in chains that keep us from being who God has called us to be. Our response can be to throw a pity party. We're called to walk through the valley, not wallow in it.

There are four steps to being set free:

1. *Trace it.*

When did it start? What events or attitudes from your past have contributed to your current state? It's time to cut it out. Cut down the root if you want to get rid of the fruit. *"Even now the ax is laid to the root of the trees. Therefore every tree which does not bear good fruit is cut down and thrown into the fire"* (Luke 3:9).

2. *Face it.*

Admit to God and to people you trust that you have a problem. Simply say, "I need help, Lord; I'm struggling with this." Whatever has been locked away needs to be brought out into the light of day.

3. *Erase it.*

Let it all go. *"If we confess our sins, He is faithful and just to forgive us our sins and to cleanse us from all unrighteousness"* (1 John 1:9). Erase all sin and offense by applying the blood of Jesus Christ.

4. *Replace it.*

Let the Holy Spirit fill the void. Ephesians 5:18 says, *"Be filled with the Spirit."* Renew your mind in the Word. Think God's thoughts, and ask God for a fresh baptism of joy. Isaiah 61:3 teaches us to put on *"the garment of praise for the spirit of heaviness."*

Remember that God will always allow a little crisis to keep us dependent. The Lord will either calm your storms or calm you while the storm rages. God can turn every Calvary into an Easter, every midnight into a noonday, every sob into a sigh. Jesus will never allow you to drown in your own tears. He will not permit hurt to destroy your mind. He bottles every tear in His eternal container. *"You number my wanderings; put my tears into Your bottle"* (Psalm 56:8).

Right now, there are women reading these words who need to be set free from the bondage of self-pity. You are a child of God filled with His Spirit. Your name is in the Book of Life. The greatest issue in your life—the sin issue—has been settled. Your sins are under the blood of Jesus.

Say this out loud, right now:

I'm through feeling sorry for myself.

God wants me to be a victor, not a victim;

to soar, not sink;

to overcome, not be overwhelmed.

Nothing outside of us can cause depression, but our unbiblical response to things can.

In Jesus' name, I break you free from the bondage of self-pity.

BREAKING FREE FROM YOUR PAST

Ezekiel 18:2 says, *"What do you mean when you use this proverb concerning the land of Israel, saying: 'The fathers have eaten sour grapes, and the children's teeth are set on edge'?"*

This text refers to the sins of parents affecting their children. The sour grapes may be an abusive father or mother. Maybe your parents didn't know how to show love. Maybe they were absent or never available to you. Perhaps you could never do well enough for them. Possibly you never received any affection or affirmation. Sour grapes could be alcoholism, drug addiction, anger, negativism, or depression. These are some of the ways parents who eat sour grapes affect their children. A good reason to throw a pity party, right?

Wrong! Look at the next verse:

"As I live," says the Lord GOD, *"you shall no longer use this proverb in Israel."*   (Ezekiel 18:3)

Good news! No matter who your father or mother is, no matter what their issues were, if Jesus is alive in you, then your parents' behavior no longer needs to become your stain. Jesus broke the curse.

No matter what sour grapes your parents ate, no matter what they did wrong, it doesn't have to destroy your joy. You don't have to be held hostage by what they did to you or didn't do for you. So many people are dealing with issues that stem from past incidents of deep rejection, sexual shame, need for approval, never feeling good enough, or lack of self-worth.

No matter how your parents behaved, through Christ, the pain stops—sin's progression in your family line is broken. To the people who know their sovereign Lord lives, this sour grape proverb is defeated. Buddha and Muhammad can't break your family curse; neither one is alive. Our sovereign Lord is alive! In Jesus' name, I loose you from the bondage of family curse and sin.

> **Life has done nothing to you that God can't use for good, if you put it in His hands.**

The assignment God has for you is too great to be sabotaged by the past. Depression and lack of self-worth is illegal in your life. Life has done nothing to you that God can't use for good, if you will put it in His hands. God can turn your pain into purpose. It's time to make a difference.

THE SECRET TO LIFE TRANSFORMATION

You are already a success in the eyes of God. What is success? Don't fall for the world's faulty definition of success: fame and fortune. True success is knowing your worth in the eyes of God, and using your gifts properly. You may be thinking, *But you don't know how I have failed.* As Edwin Cole once said, "You don't drown by falling into the water; you drown by staying there."

The book of Romans tells us that the renewing of the mind is the secret to transformation. (See Romans 12:2.) What you see and believe in your mind, you will live out. Believe you are victorious. See yourself making a difference. If you know who you are, and Who has called you, you will be able to endure anything. *"Who for the joy that was set before Him endured the cross"* (Hebrews 12:2). Jesus set His mind on the victory while He endured the crucifixion.

My mother-in-law, Pat, is a breast cancer survivor. My wife and I will never forget hearing the news. *Cancer* is a devastating word, especially when it is attached to someone you love. After a few tears and a lot of prayer, Pat began to fight back. She refused to give up. Although the doctors recommended radical mastectomy surgery, she decided on the alternate route, a strict diet and immune-boosting vitamins.

I felt the call of God to fast three days for her healing. On the third day, God gave me a word of encouragement for her: "You shall live to see your children's children." Pat has now been cancer-free for over fourteen years! After going through such a storm, every day is like a gift. Today, she has turned her liability into an asset by encouraging other women with her testimony. Through the test came a testimony; from the mess came a message of hope for others walking through the emotional meat grinder of cancer.

The reason some people are never used by God is that they have never been through anything. God gets His best sailors from the roughest seas and His fiercest soldiers from the toughest battles. God can use what you have experienced to bless others.

Such was the case in the life of Sylina LiBasci. I felt impressed to share with you a portion of her personal testimony about the most devastating day of her life:

> On May 16, 1997, I was being a mom as usual, and I got up early enough to have my devotion and pray. My four-year-old son, Caleb, came in, and I bathed him. Soon, my two-year-old, Benjamin, was awake, so I bathed him. I fed them breakfast while Wesli, my ten-year-old daughter, was dressing for the day.

We were planning a day of fun at our church: water day at our Parents Morning Out class. I taught it on Fridays. The boys wanted to wear their "Jesus" shirts. These pictured Jesus with children and the Scripture from Matthew 19:14, which read, *"Let the little children come to Me, and do not forbid them; for of such is the kingdom of heaven."* They were so eager that morning. I had no way of knowing this would be our last morning together.

On the way to church, a dump truck struck our car. My four-year-old, Caleb, went to be with Jesus instantly. Benjamin was critically injured and lived only two days and sixteen hours after the accident. My daughter, Wesli, was taken from the scene by helicopter to a children's hospital where, thankfully, she fully recovered from her injuries.

Though I will never fully understand why God chose to take my children, I can say God has turned my crisis into a miracle. The driver of the truck that struck us asked Jesus into his heart. Many doctors and nurses told us they would never be the same. But the greatest miracle occurred at the memorial service—where sixteen of our family members accepted Christ.

We had been praying for a household revival, and this was the beginning. God has opened the doors for us to minister to many grieving families. We have seen the Lord bind up the brokenhearted through our hardest life experience.

Although Sylina and her husband faced the greatest tragedy of their lives, God was able to bring something good out of it. Nothing can ever take the place of the children that she lost, but she takes comfort in knowing a difference has been made in the lives of others who are hurting, and one day she will see them again.

I can promise you, hell is frightened that you're reading this book. New orders have come out of hell: "Don't let women catch a word of what's in that book. Don't let them understand what travailing prayer can do. Don't let them pick up on a spirit of discernment. Let the women stay so burdened with problems, so full of inferiority and self-pity, that they will never discover their gift of discernment and learn what a vital role they play in Satan's defeat."

The enemy fears praying, discerning women! They can break his authority over the home, over the family, over the husband, over the children. And when he's lost those battles, he's lost the war!

Chapter Eleven

THE DISCERNING MAN IS A REAL MAN

Behold, I will send you Elijah the prophet
before the coming of the great and dreadful day of the
LORD. And he will turn the hearts of the fathers to the
children, and the hearts of the children to their fathers.
—Malachi 4:5–6

What a powerful Scripture this is; it's really a warning. It may be the Old Testament, but the truth that it refers to affects us, particularly in this generation. It was saying, in effect, "Before the coming of the Messiah, there will be a turning of the hearts of the fathers back to their children."

There is a difference between being a male and being a man. Just because you're a male, that doesn't make you a man.

What is a real man? You don't measure a real man by muscles, but by moral fiber! You don't measure a real man by how successful he is in business, but by how successful he is at home! No amount of career success will compensate for failure at home. There's a difference between your reputation and your character. Reputation is who people *think* you are. Character is who your wife and your children *know* you are.

Real marriage has to go beyond moonlight and roses to daylight and dishes. Real marriage has to go beyond sex to sensitivity. Real marriage has to go beyond romance to responsibility. Statistics tell us that in homes where the father is a committed Christian, the children have a 75 percent chance of growing up to become committed Christians themselves. But in homes where only the mother is a committed Christian, that number drops to 23 percent. It's very obvious. God needs our males to stand up and become discerning men of God in the home.

> Reputation is who people think you are. Character is who your family knows you are.

When Joshua and the nation of Israel stood just across the river from their long-awaited Promised Land, God spoke to Joshua, saying, in effect, "Joshua, tomorrow I'm going to take you across the river. Tomorrow, forty years of waiting is coming to an end; you're going to walk into a land flowing with milk and honey." But God had one last instruction for Joshua. *"Make flint knives for yourself, and circumcise the sons of Israel again the second time"* (Joshua 5:2). He was basically saying, "Sanctify them again." As every man surely knows, circumcision was a cutting of the flesh that designated Jewish men as set apart to be used by God. Now, before Israel could enter their Promised Land, God was calling for a re-sanctification.

BECOMING RE-SANCTIFIED

God was saying, "Unprecedented blessings are about to come to My people. But before I can take their families into all that I have prepared for them, I need the men to be re-sanctified. There needs to be a cutting away of fleshly things."

The truth is, you've been getting by while carrying some fleshly things. You've been doing some things thinking that God will just sort of wink at it—"Boys will be boys." But God is saying something different. He's saying, in effect, "This new thing I want to do requires a resanctification in every man's life. I want their eyes to be sanctified. I want their hearts to be sanctified. I want their minds and their spirits to be pure. I don't want them just coming to church and taking a secondary role in spiritual things in the home."

Circumcision, of course, was a cutting in those hidden, sensitive places. And that's just where men need it. We need to deal with those secret issues, those fleshly things, that are hanging on to us, hindering us from receiving God's unprecedented blessings!

You probably know the story of Passover found in Exodus, where God killed all the firstborn of Egypt, but spared, or "passed over," the Israelite homes that had a marking on the door. In Ezekiel 9, there is an example of another Passover:

> *The LORD said to him, "Go through the midst of the city, through the midst of Jerusalem, and put a mark on the foreheads of the men who sigh and cry over all the abominations that are done within it." To the others He said in my hearing, "Go after him through the city and kill; do not let your eye spare, nor have any pity....But do not come near anyone on whom is the mark."* (Ezekiel 9:4–6)

The application is this: God is saying, "If I can find men who will be burdened and cry out to Me for their wives and children, I'll save their families. But if there's not a man in that house who will carry the burden, then the destroyer will slay the women and the children."

I propose to you that we're living in just such days when the devourer is targeting our children and our wives. There may have been a time when you could get by with being secondary, spiritually; with allowing your wife to do the praying and the Bible reading and the spiritual stuff, but we're living in an hour when I believe God is marking homes. He's saying, "There needs to be a man in every home who knows how to cry out, who knows how to pray for himself." Your pastor is not the spiritual head of your home; you are. And it's time for you to cry aloud. It's time for you to mark your home for the blessing.

GROW UP INTO DISCERNMENT

In 1 Corinthians 13:11, Paul said, *"When I was a child, I spoke as a child, I understood as a child, I thought as a child; but when I became a man, I put away childish things."* Notice that Paul used *when* twice. There's the *"when"* of childhood and the *"when"* of manhood. He's not talking about your physical age, how many years you've been on this earth. There are some men out there who are locked in a protracted state of childhood. Children act like children. *"But when I became a man...."* It's time for some of you to grow up.

There comes a time, a right of passage, when you move from childhood to manhood. People who know you should be able to look at you a year from now and see that you've got bigger faith, bigger commitment, a bigger prayer life, and bigger dedication to God.

Unfortunately, some men are stuck in spiritual childhood. You've been coming to church for a year, two years, maybe more, and by now, your children ought to see Daddy praising the Lord and discerning the things of God. Instead, you're still arguing about tithes, wondering whether you're going to go to church or not, and watching television or surfing the Internet instead of reading God's Word. I'm saying to you, man to man, it's time for the men of God to grow up! Hell has targeted your home and God is looking for discerning men who will cry out to Him for their families!

> There are wounds only a father can cause, and wounds only a father can heal!

Notice, Paul said, *"I put away childish things."* He didn't say, "God took them away." Paul had to do some things for himself. God is saying, "I'm ready to mature you. I'm ready to take you to a new level!" In Malachi, He said, in effect, "I'm going to turn the hearts of the fathers back to the children." There are wounds in us that only a father can cause; there are wounds in us that only a father can heal!

CURSE OF THE FATHERLESS

Kruger National Park in South Africa is the largest game preserve in the world. When they were facing an overpopulation of elephants, they decided to separate the younger elephants because they were eating all the vegetation. So they took three hundred of the younger male elephants, separated them from the influence of the older, mature elephants, and moved them to South Africa's Hluhluwe-Umfolozi Reserve, three hundred miles away.

Hluhluwe-Umfolozi had no elephants but happened to be the natural terrain of the rare white rhino. The rhino has no natural enemies. It's not prey for anything. It's too mean, too tough, too fast, too strong. But to the amazement of authorities, they began to find dead rhinos all over the park. They couldn't figure out why. So they put cameras up and found that these young, male elephants, with no mature influence in their lives, were forming into packs and gangs to kill rhinos—something that was not in their nature.

Every night on the news, in every city in America, there are stories of gang violence. Do you know why we've got gangs roaming? Do you know why we've got killing and shooting? I believe it's because we don't have older, mature men who are speaking into the lives of our younger men, mentoring and developing and maturing and teaching them what is acceptable behavior and what is unacceptable.

Isaiah 4:1 gives a dire prediction: *"In that day seven women will take hold of one man and say, 'We will eat our own food and provide our own clothes; only let us be called by your name. Take away our disgrace!'"* (NIV). I believe this is a prophecy of the last days when there will be such a shortage of mature, discerning, godly men that women will come, seven women to one man, with their families, not for marriage or anything immoral, but for shelter, because they won't be able to find enough godly men to speak over their children and over their families' lives. Perhaps as the prophet said this, he foresaw our situation today, when 50 percent of the children in the U.S. are growing up in fatherless homes.

MEN AND WOMEN ARE DIFFERENT

If you know anything about biology, you know that when a man and woman conceive a child, the woman always

142

provides an "X" chromosome because it's all she has. The male has both "X" and "Y" chromosomes. If he provides an "X," the child becomes a girl. If he provides a "Y," the child becomes a boy. The female doesn't have the ability to determine the sex of the child. It is the male that gives that identity to the child. If this is true in the natural world, think about the influence of a father to give identity to his children in the spiritual world. Nobody can speak into the life of our children like a man can. That's why it's so important for you to understand your role as a husband and father. A fatherless generation is being raised, but they've never been told who they are by a strong, male, godly voice!

Which chromosome we get makes so much difference in who we eventually become. Ladies, when you get that "X" chromosome, you get a stronger immune system, and because of that you will live, on average, eight years longer than men. Studies prove that women fare better than men in concentration camps. Women withstand pain better than men. Women's cells only deteriorate 2 percent every ten years, while men's cells deteriorate 10 percent in the same time.

Men, on the other hand, have some benefits with their "Y" chromosome. Men carry a gallon and a half of blood in their bodies, compared to a woman's four-fifths of a gallon. A man has over one million more red blood cells per drop than a woman. That's why men have more physical strength.

Perhaps the greatest difference between men and women is in how our brains are wired. At conception, males and females are basically identical. But after a number of days, the male genes trigger the release of the chemical testosterone. The moment this chemical washes over the brain of the male child, it destroys some of the connecting fibers between its left and right side. However, an equivalent testosterone wash does not occur in the developing female's brain, and the left and right sides of her brain stay connected. This shows that men are literally brain damaged at birth! The frying of some of the connective fibers between the right and left sides of the brain causes the man to be linear in his thinking. He uses only one side of the brain at a time. It's a medical fact.

Women think using both sides of the brain. They're like radar all the time, noticing everything. Men, on the other hand, are more logical, trying to make A plus B equal C. Women, on average, are more sensitive than men, sensitive to sound and light, as well as emotions.

Men use the left side of the brain most of the time. This is the side of the brain that is challenge-oriented, focused on objectives and goals. The right side of the brain is more feeling-oriented, nurture-oriented. It is better at remembering.

My point is this: God made us different for a reason. As great and gifted as women are, we need the influence of men in our homes, as well, to provide balance, stability, and protection. If you're a single mother, you need your church to provide strong male leadership for your children. The Lord said, *"Turn the hearts of the fathers to the children"* (Malachi 4:6). But He's also saying, "I need some men who'll carry a burden, some men who will be willing to say, 'Lord, I'm Yours.'"

THERE'S A DAD IN THE HOUSE

Men, if a young man is coming to date your daughter, your silence is consent. Put down the remote control; turn off ESPN. You need to meet him at the door. He needs to know that this girl he's with has a daddy who's going to be watching. You need to look him in the eye and say, "Who are you? Who are your parents? What church do you go to? Where are you going to eat? And what time exactly will you be leaving and what time will you be home?"

You need to go down to the school and meet the principal and the teachers. They need to know that there's a daddy who cares. That's what a father does. There's more to being a man than bringing home a paycheck. Anyone can do that.

Men, we've gotten lazy and lethargic. We have to get into our children's world! We have to know what's going on! We have to develop our spiritual discernment in order to feel when things aren't right in our household!

If your marriage is going to pieces and you're growing more and more distant, you need to open up your mouth and communicate. You need to say something. You need to do something to break the ice. You need to reach out; that's what men do. To be manly is to be godly.

> **Men must develop spiritual discernment to feel when things aren't right in the household.**

Why are you so quiet? Open up your mouth and talk to God about your family. Talk to Him about your marriage. To be silent is to give consent. If you're silent, then God will be silent. But if you'll start praying, God will start moving. If you'll start speaking, God will start speaking. Use your voice and speak into your family blessing, identity, and anointing, in Jesus' name. Stand up and say, like Joshua, *"As for me and my house, we will serve the LORD"* (Joshua 24:15)!

THE SPIRIT OF A MAN

Proverbs 20:27 says, *"The spirit of a man is the lamp of the LORD; searching all the inner depths of his heart."* I have always interpreted that Scripture to mean that when God leads us, He does so through our spirits. He doesn't talk to our minds; He talks to our spirits, because *"the spirit of a man is the lamp of the LORD."*

This verse always makes me wonder, *What kind of light does my spirit give off?* That's a question we all need to ask ourselves, especially since our spirits are the lamp of the Lord. God, who is light, says, in effect, "The only light I have on earth to invade the darkness is the spirits of men and women."

In 2 Samuel 16, we find the story of David, whose throne has been overthrown by his son, Absalom. Scripture tells us,

> *Now when King David came to Bahurim, there was a man…whose name was Shimei the son of Gera, coming from there. He came out, cursing continuously as he came. And he threw stones at David and at all the servants of King David. And all the people and all the mighty men were on his right hand and on his left. Also Shimei said thus when he cursed: "Come out! Come out! You bloodthirsty man, you rogue!"* (2 Samuel 16:5–7)

David and his thirty mighty men were leaving their homes and their families, running for their lives. They were leaving everything they owned behind. These were warriors, but they were angry and embarrassed because not only have they lost everything, but now this little pipsqueak named Shimei threw rocks and cursed them as they left town.

One of the men turned and pleaded with David, *"Why should this dead dog curse my lord the king? Please, let me go over and take off his head!"* (2 Samuel 16:9). You can almost see the veins popping on his forehead, his hand on the shaft of his sword, just dying to go and take care of the nuisance. But David said,

> *Let him alone, and let him curse; for so the LORD has ordered him. It may be that the LORD will look on my affliction, and that the LORD will repay me with good for his cursing this day.* (2 Samuel 16:11–12)

David said, in effect, "This could be God checking me out, taking His lamp and putting it on my spirit to see what kind of spirit I really have."

Power withholding itself is far greater than power exerting itself. A Man proved that on a cross two thousand years ago. As He was arrested in the garden of Gethsemane, Jesus could have called down ten thousand angels, but He refused to do so. (See Matthew 26:53.) Imagine David looking at this little man who wasn't worthy to shine his shoes and basically saying, "I believe God is checking out my spirit in this situation."

THE TRIAL OF PRESSURE

There will be times when God will allow trial, complaint, and maybe even false accusation to come into your life. At that moment, God will take His lamp and put it to your spirit. You may be stronger and have more power and influence than your accuser. You may be able to crush him. But God knows that who you are under pressure is who you are. God wants to see if you've got the right spirit in the face of adversity. God wants to know if you are able to *"bless those who curse you, and pray for those who spitefully use you"* (Luke 6:28).

It is in times of pressure, times of crisis, that your real spirit will come out. I love to walk with men who possess a good spirit. You may not be perfect. You may mess up. You may do things wrong. But God always goes beneath the surface to illuminate our spirits, saying, in effect, "I want to see how much light you're putting off by your spirit." No matter what happens to you in life; no matter who hurts you; no matter who cuts you off in traffic or undermines you at work; no matter what happens in your marriage or in your home, you need to have God's spirit, not a bitter, unforgiving, and angry spirit.

THE SPIRIT OF JESUS

The night before the crucifixion, an argument arose between the apostles as to who would be the greatest in heaven. (See Luke 22:24.) It wasn't the first time this argument had arose. (See Luke 9:46.) Then, knowing He was going to the cross in the next twenty-four hours, Jesus got up, took a basin of water and a towel, and went around the table, washing the feet of His disciples. (See John 13:4–5.) He even washed the feet of Judas, who was about to leave to betray Him. I can't imagine what I would have done when I came to Judas, knowing, as Jesus did, of his upcoming betrayal. I probably would have yelled at Judas, pleaded with him, or restrained him. Instead, Jesus washed the feet of the man who would sell Him out. Jesus was demonstrating for them, beyond what words could ever say, the spirit of a servant. Then He instructed them, *"If I then, your Lord and Teacher, have washed your feet, you also ought to wash one another's feet"* (verse 14).

> Power withholding itself is far greater than power exerting itself.

"The spirit of a man is the lamp of the LORD." How much light do you give off by your spirit, by your attitude, and by who you

are on the inside? Are you angry and bitter? Do you have that kind of spirit? Or, do you project the Spirit of Jesus?

Scripture says that when we get to heaven, God will judge *"the spirits of just men made perfect"* (Hebrews 12:23). That word *perfect* doesn't mean you are perfect; it means you are *mature* in Christ. It means, even when people curse you, you move on. When you have the chance to get back at someone who has really tried to do you harm, you hold back. I don't care how much people offend you; you need to get over it. The desire of the heart of a man of God says, "Make me like Jesus. Give me the spirit of forgiveness. Give me the spirit of purity. Give me the spirit of holiness. Give me the spirit of love. Give me the Spirit of Jesus."

Part IV

BENEFITS OF DISCERNMENT

Chapter Twelve

UNMASKING THE MARRIAGE ASSASSINS

Remember the Lord, great and awesome,
and fight for your brethren, your sons, your daughters,
your wives, and your houses.

—Nehemiah 4:14

As the senior pastor of a large church, who also has the privilege of reaching millions more through a television ministry, I like to think that God has blessed me with a certain amount of spiritual discernment. But I have learned that when it comes to applying that discernment to relationships, I am not even in the same league as my wife. And without generalizing too much, most men that I know would say the same thing.

On different occasions through the years, my wife has simply been able to sense a vibe from someone who was up to no good. Sometimes she would feel uneasy about certain women who were trying to get close to me. Other times she would feel uncomfortable around men whom she sensed were making advances toward her or one of our girls. Two things have become very clear to me on this: (1) almost every time she was right on the money; and (2) I usually didn't have a clue. I've learned the hard way that when my wife whispers, "watch that one"—I had better heed the warning.

THE INTIMACY GAP

According to Dr. Tim Clinton, president of the American Association of Christian Counselors and publisher of the award-winning magazine *Christian Counseling Today*, 67 percent of all women will experience one or more premarital or extramarital affairs in their lifetimes. Some experts believe this percentage is much higher. Why are so many women struggling with extramarital affairs? Many of these women are tempted because their husbands do not meet their emotional needs.

Women crave emotional intimacy in the same way that men crave physical intimacy. Consequently, just as men are vulnerable to unfaithfulness in the absence of sex, women are vulnerable to unfaithfulness in the absence of emotional connection. Men tend to give love to get sex; women tend to give sex to get love. Men are stimulated by what they see, where women are stimulated by what they hear. Think of the word *intimacy* as "into-me-see." It is both physical and emotional.

THE PATH TO DESTRUCTION

Nobody would have an affair if he or she could see where it would ultimately lead. We must strip away the deceptive disguise in which sexual immorality cloaks itself. To David, sin wrapped itself in the body of the beautiful woman, Bathsheba, as he watched her bathe. But he could not see beyond the steamy sexual affair to the devastating effects that his adultery would breed: a husband killed, a baby dead, a daughter raped by her brother, and a son killed by his brother. Adultery always seems exciting and titillating, but always brings pain, grief, and sorrow.

If only he could have stripped away the beauty of Delilah, Samson would have seen beyond her disguise to what sin never wants to show. He would have seen how the strongest man in the nation would end up imprisoned, blind, and a slave. Samson learned that sin has a binding effect, a blinding effect, and a grinding effect. What a fall for a man who was once a strong man of God. Chalk up another victim fallen prey to lust.

> Deception is Satan's number one weapon, and discernment is our number one defense.

Sexual sin only shows you the excitement and immediate gratification; it never shows you the brokenhearted children of divorce. It never shows you the sexually transmitted diseases that ravage the body. Satan only shows you the prodigal son's hotel suite, never his pigpen. Satan only shows you his entrance, never the exit.

Sin never says, "Here's what I really am." Sin must constantly change its wardrobe so it won't be recognized. Deception is Satan's number one weapon, and discernment must be our number one defense.

Far too often, we put on our best religious masks to wear to church, wanting to look our very best with our religious façades. All the while, serious marital problems hide beneath the surface, which are crying out to be revealed and healed.

Such masks become assassins that can kill what looked on the outside to be a perfect marriage.

Let's strip off the disguise and unmask twelve marriage assassins that could be targeting your marriage.

Marriage Assassin #1
A long marriage is a secure marriage.

That's like saying, "Just because you have lived a long time, you're physically healthy right now." Not necessarily. You can develop false security thinking that, because you've been married for many years, your marriage is safe.

Statistics show an increasing ratio of divorce among people married twenty-five years or more. After all those years of chasing children and career, both husband and wife can suddenly find themselves going in opposite directions. They have nothing in common anymore but the children. Once the children head off to college, they discover they are strangers under the same roof. The common ground they once shared is gone.

The sad thing about divorce is that you separate before you divorce. Years before the actual divorce, silent erosion, like waves on the seashore, slowly washes away the love. Your marriage can experience significant erosion through the years.

Anything that is not fed will die. To foster a healthy marriage there must be "maintenance" of the marriage. Christians often live under the illusion that divorce can't happen to them. But as they spend less and less time with each other, the marriage spark slowly extinguishes. It is foolish to think that, as long as you come home every night and occasionally have sexual relations with your mate, you have a good marriage.

Death rarely comes suddenly. First there are symptoms, which lead to more sickness, which then leads to death. Likewise, destruction in a marriage follows a progression. A weak marriage becomes a sick marriage; a sick marriage left unattended will die. Don't wait until your marriage dies. Heed the warning signs. It's too late to call a lifeguard after someone has already drowned.

Do you want a good marriage? Pay attention to it. Now is the time to rescue your marriage.

Marriage Assassin #2

Selfishness and a preoccupation with *you*.

Some time ago, I was traveling with my wife and three oldest daughters. It was getting late, and I was ready to get home. My wife asked me to stop at a store and get her a Coke to drink. Any other time, I would have been glad to accommodate her, but the store was on the other side of the highway, it was late, and I was tired. Besides, we were only a few miles from the house, and there was plenty to drink there. I decided to drive right past the store.

You could have cut the atmosphere with a knife. Cherise didn't speak another word to me the rest of the ride home. The girls wisely sat silent in the backseat. As I got out of the car at home, I heard an ice-cold voice say, "Leave the keys in the car." As we got out, my wife burned rubber going out of the driveway. (She really wanted that Coke!) I learned a great lesson over the next three or four days of receiving the cold shoulder. If she wants a Coke, buy her that Coke! I've learned to always keep a case on hand.

Marriage requires us to put the other person first constantly. The job description for a husband is found in

Ephesians 5:25: *"Husbands, love your wives, just as Christ also loved the church and gave Himself for her."* It can be summed up in one word—*sacrifice*. The job description of a wife is found in Ephesians 5:22: *"Wives, submit to your own husbands as to the Lord."* It can be summed up in one word also—*submit*, which means "to show honor." We need to get ourselves in gear and start sacrificing and submitting one to another.

Be careful not to make it all about you. Recognize the signs if everything becomes about what *you* have to have and what *you're* not getting out of the relationship. Nobody gets divorced worrying about what his or her spouse needs. Remember, the word *sin* has an "I" right in the middle of it. Beware of the "me, myself, and I" spirit.

Marriage Assassin #3
Immaturity

I am seven years older than my wife. I told her that I wanted to marry someone who could push my wheelchair very fast when I get old! Our age difference presented some unique challenges early in our marriage. Cherise was just eighteen years old when I married her. She thought being married to an evangelist meant living a carefree life as we traveled from city to city. She envisioned sightseeing during the day and dressing up at night for church. It sounds like fun, doesn't it? After about three months of almost nonstop travel and going to church almost every night, Cherise was through. She was sick of living in hotel rooms.

It all came to a head in Washington, D.C. I was preaching a revival at a church, and she informed me that she was bored, and getting tired of going to church all the time. She said that she wanted to go home to her mother. After a heated discussion, she left the room. That's right; I also married a runaway bride. For hours I searched for her throughout the hotel. I called her mother, and we were both in tears worrying about her. It was getting close to church time, and I was about to have a nervous breakdown. I didn't know if something had happened to her, or if she had been kidnapped. It turns out she had gone into the gift shop at the hotel and bought some magazines to read. Then she went into the laundry room of the hotel to avoid me.

As you can imagine, by the time that I got to church that night, I was a wreck. Cherise still laughs about how I requested prayer from the congregation because "I had been fighting the devil all day long!"

We worked through our problems. Looking back, I realize how hard it was for my eighteen-year-old wife to suddenly have to seem so mature. Eventually, I learned to take time off, and she learned that life is not always a bed of roses. We both grew up—sort of. However, I still occasionally feel like "I'm fighting the devil all day long." I'm sure Cherise occasionally pines for an "easier life." Pray for us, saints. Pray!

Immaturity is when somebody in the marriage refuses to grow up. Remember the wise words of 1 Corinthians 13:11. *"When I was a child, I spoke as a child, I understood as a child, I thought as a child; but when I became a man, I put away childish things."* There comes a time when temper tantrums and pouting must cease.

Marriage Assassin #4
Manipulation

Manipulation in marriage occurs when you think you are so wonderful, and the only reason you married your mate was to straighten him or her out. Deep down inside you think you need to fix your mate, to change him or her into the person your mate should be. Often, you're trying to make your mate just like you, and, truth be told, you don't even like you!

In a loving marriage relationship, sometimes you do things because your partner wants to do them. You go places because your partner wants to go. You enjoy certain things because he or she enjoys them. Not so in the manipulative marriage relationship, where one partner tries to change the other into what the partner wants him or her to be, instead of what God made that person to be.

Marriage Assassin #5
Lack of Commitment

Your mate needs to know, regardless of what happens, you will not leave him or her. Maybe at the marriage altar you said your vows to a svelte, 32-inch waist, but now he's a paunchy, 44-inch waist. Maybe he married a size 8, but now he's married to a size 18. Marriage is a commitment regardless of the changes the relationships—or the people in them—undergo. Remember those vows: "For richer or poorer, in sickness and in health, until death do us part."

I heard the story of a university president in South Carolina whose wife was stricken with Alzheimer's. Every day this man would sit by her bedside and read stories to her. Eventually, he decided to resign his prestigious position at the university in order to spend more time with her. Upon his resignation, one of the board members asked him why he was resigning, saying, "Your wife doesn't even know who you are." His response was classic: "Fifty years ago, I made a commitment to her, and though she may not know who I am, I know who she is."

In an uncommitted society, one of the keys to happiness is costly commitment.

Marriage Assassin #6
Promiscuity

We live in a sex-driven society. Everywhere you look the media is bombarding us with more sex. Modern technology has opened vast avenues of opportunities for someone looking for companionship, understanding, or sex. Pornography, cybersex, webcams, and chat rooms have drawn millions into their clutches by giving the illusion that they are offering exactly what you're missing.

The reality of marriage simply cannot compete with the temporary thrill of casual affairs, or with the fantasy of the Internet. In an affair, you see only the best of the other person. You do not wash their underwear; you just watch them take it on and off. But when you get married, you see the other person, warts and all. You discover that marriage breathes in and out, and has its ups and downs.

> The reality of marriage can't compete with the fantasy of the Internet.

There are three levels of love in every marriage:

Hot love: The sex is great. It's wild, fun, and free! Your marriage can't operate at the hot love level all the time. Hot love is much like the cheetah I mentioned before—it is fast, but cannot sustain.

Warm Love: You've been married a while, and you've delivered a few kids. You're both running all over the place taking care of the kids and working to build your careers. Consequently, you're both tired and busy, so naturally things begin to cool in the relationship.

Cold love: This includes a season of diminished sexual relations. Sometimes it stems from friction in the marriage, and sometimes it is because of physical illness or limitations, but cold love is the most important love because it's covenant love. It's based on a commitment to each other, no matter what.

All marriages will exhibit all three of these temperatures. The reason cold love is the most significant is that when you have mastered cold love, the other two temperatures always come back. A marriage moves from hot love to warm love to cold love, but if you are committed to each other it will not always stay cold. It will once again go back to the hot love you once knew.

Marriage Assassin #7
Stress

When both the husband and wife are working and have no time for each other, stress can assassinate the marriage. I recommend a date night once a week, where you and your spouse get away from everybody and everything just to spend time together. Maybe going out to dinner and watching a movie is an idea you would enjoy with your mate.

At times, your mate may be so burned out from stress that you have to pull him or her out of the fire. You may revive the enjoyable person who has been hiding inside of your mate when you escort him or her away for an evening of relaxation and romance.

Marriage Assassin #8
Economic Pressure

Arguing about money can destroy your marriage. The thing that brought you together didn't have anything to do with money. When you were first married, life was all about being together. It's so easy to lose sight of that.

For many marriages, I highly recommend plastic surgery. That's when you cut up those plastic credit cards that are charging you 18 percent interest. Put yourself on a budget. Don't try to keep up with the Joneses, because by the time you've finally caught up, they will have refinanced!

Marriage Assassin #9
Outside Interference

Don't allow your mother or your mother-in-law, your ex-spouse, your best friend, your children, associates on the job, or third parties to come between you and your mate. The Bible says to leave and cleave. *"For this reason a man shall leave his father and mother and be joined to his wife, and the two shall become one flesh"* (Matthew 19:5).

Psalm 1:1 says, *"Blessed is the man who walks not in the counsel of the ungodly."* Never allow ungodly people to counsel you about your marriage. Beware of outside interference.

Marriage Assassin #10
Unforgiveness

In a marriage, a spirit of forgiveness must operate continually. Every time you get in an argument, are you the kind of person who reaches back and brings up old dirt? If you are, then you are sabotaging your marriage.

You can't change what has happened in the past. So, you need to admit it, quit it, and forget it. All you have left is the future, so commit to building your future together. Be quick to forgive. You may say, "But they haven't asked me to forgive them yet." Jesus forgave on the cross before His murderers asked. He prayed, *"Father, forgive them for they do not know what they do"* (Luke 23:34).

Marriage Assassin #11
Comparing

Constantly comparing your spouse to others is very unhealthy for your relationship. "I wish my wife looked that good." "My husband just doesn't meet my emotional needs like her husband does." "I wish my spouse would go to church on Sunday like theirs do."

Before you know it, you are convinced that the grass must be greener on the other side. Comparing your spouse to others can lead to fantasies about being with another man or woman.

Let's face it. There will always be someone better looking, smarter, and more successful than your husband. There will always be someone prettier, thinner, and smarter than your wife. Second Corinthians 10:12 says, *"They, measuring themselves by themselves, and comparing themselves among themselves, are not wise."*

Do you fantasize about being intimate with someone else? Do you converse with strangers in Internet chat rooms?

"What does a little fantasy hurt?" you say.

Just as you would be offended if your spouse's eyes wandered, your spouse has a right to be offended when your mind wanders. It is okay to fantasize if the fantasy is restricted to your marriage partner; otherwise, fantasizing is mental and emotional unfaithfulness.

Marriage Assassin #12
The Wrong Environment

Many times, when people fall morally it's because they allowed themselves to be in the wrong place at the wrong time. Second Samuel 11:1–2 says, *"At the time when kings go out to battle...David remained at Jerusalem...and walked on the roof of the king's house."* This Scripture describes the evening when David saw Bathsheba bathing. He was in the wrong place at the wrong time. You have to be able to discern when you are on the ledge of lust. It's dangerous to be alone in the wrong place with the wrong person.

Avoid "bedroom settings." You have the chemistry for anything to happen; I don't care how spiritual you are. Married or single, the key is to not put yourself in situations where you have no business being.

A blind man will always be at an advantage in a dark room. Why? It is because you are on his turf. If a blind man wants to beat you up, all he has to do is turn the lights off. Satan is the prince of darkness, so he tries to entice you into the darkness where he has the advantage. Stay off his turf!

Remember, sexual sin always disguises itself at first. It may begin with a "harmless" emotional bond or friendship with someone of the opposite sex. As it progresses, a mental stronghold of lust will develop. Before you know it, every morning when you get dressed you choose your attire based on trying to be attractive to him or her.

This is dangerous on many levels and can work against you in your employment as well as your marriage. In the workplace, be careful. It is wise to keep doors open in the office when you are meeting with people of the opposite sex. Even a casual hug can lead to misunderstanding. If you are married, you should never ride in a car alone or go to lunch alone with someone of the opposite sex. The devil does not have the authority to tempt you beyond what you are able to bear (see 1 Corinthians 10:13), but if you get in the wrong setting, the need to connect intimately with someone will take over. Save your intimate affection for your immediate family only.

Decide what your principles are before you ever get into a tempting situation. Build your "hedge" before circumstances go awry. (See Job 1:10.) That way, when the temptation comes, you have already made the decision. If you have to wait until a crisis comes to make up your mind about how you'll behave, it's too late. If a voice on the inside says, *Something is not right about this setting,* listen to it. When confronted with a tempting situation, be like Joseph in Genesis 39:15—run!

Today, a happy home, a good marriage, and a loving family are endangered species. There are fewer and fewer traditional families. The divorce rates continue to rise, and the number of unmarried couples cohabiting keeps soaring. Sadly, when the family splits up, the chances of the children serving God are diminished greatly.

The two greatest institutions on earth are the family and the church, which is why Satan targets them both. If the home is the number one priority of the devil and his marriage assassins, you better make it your number one priority!

I'm very concerned with the devaluing of the sacred vows of marriage. Nehemiah 4:14 says, *"Fight for your brethren, your sons, your daughters, your wives, and your houses."* Your loved ones are a cause worth fighting for. Fight for your family! Strong families produce a strong church and a strong nation.

You can't afford to play around with sexual sin. You can't afford to compromise your convictions. If you do, your children and your children's children will be adversely affected. You have to stand firm on the Word. Surround yourself with high moral standards and strong personal convictions. We know how human nature is—once you start letting down the standards, you open up the gate. If you don't want to commit adultery, then don't return that look or that wink. *"Abstain from every form of evil"* (1 Thessalonians 5:22).

> The greatest institutions on earth are the family and the church, which is why Satan targets them both.

Sometimes you may feel pressure to be nice to people who are acting out of line and asking you to compromise your standards. You may say, "If I tell them to stop, they will think I'm being rude."

You are not being rude; you are being faithful to your mate and to God. Are you in a pressure situation at work? Your personal standards can affect future generations of your family. *"For I, the LORD your God, am a jealous God, visiting the iniquity of the fathers upon the children to the third and fourth generations of those who hate Me"* (Exodus 20:5).

God has standards; He has set limits and boundaries for us. We are not of this world. Our obligation to God is to be a light on a hill, not to fade into the darkness. (See Matthew 5:14.)

Ask the Lord for strength in these areas of your marriage. Simply ask, "Lord, give me the guts to stand for what is right! Even if it costs me, even if I feel pressure from the top to compromise, help me to remember that some things are just not for sale. Thank You, Lord."

Chapter Thirteen

DISCERNING SEXUAL TEMPTATION

For this is the will of God, your sanctification:
that you should abstain from sexual immorality.
—1 Thessalonians 4:3

I suggest that every parent reading this book share this chapter with their teenagers. We are living in a society where young girls and boys are asked to become adults overnight. Many young people have been trained to think that once they have sex, they will be "real" men and women; until then, they are merely little boys and girls.

"Girls Gone Wild" seems to be the moral theme of our current times. The twisted sexual images pop culture continues to produce, promoting everything from homosexual experimentation to casual sex, are in direct contradiction with God's Word.

The negative influences of the media, music, movies, and fashion magazines are brainwashing a generation of young men and women into believing it is perfectly normal to be sexually active before marriage.

"It's no big deal," "Everyone does it," "It can't be wrong if it feels so right," are the responses of men and women, young and old, who are making wrong decisions that seem right to them. Proverbs 14:12 says, *There is a way that seems right to a man, but its end is the way of death.*"

You must remember that even "good Christians" are not exempt from temptation. Often it is the "good" kids, kids who say they know sexual intercourse is wrong, asking, "How far can I go sexually?" When it comes to sexual integrity, most people want a list of dos and don'ts. What they really want to know is, "What can I get away with?"

What is the answer to, "How far can I go sexually?" It depends on your destination. The destination determines the route. If you want to reach God's divine plan for your life, then I would remind you of 2 Timothy 2:22, *"Flee also youthful lusts."*

Many teens today believe that anything short of sexual intercourse is okay. This is deception. It is shocking to know we live in a society where young girls are dared by their "friends" to perform oral sex in the back of school buses, and even more shocking to realize they are doing it. Could this be because society has tried to convince us that oral sex is not "real sex"?

CHANGING SEXUAL MORALS

In 1998, President Bill Clinton claimed he did not have sexual relations with Monica Lewinsky. He claimed that oral sex was not technically having sex. While his accusers didn't buy his argument, unfortunately many young people did. According to the 1999 fall issue of *Seventeen* magazine, of 723 male and female teens, ages 15–19, 49 percent considered oral sex inferior to sexual intercourse; 40 percent said that it did not count as sex.

Sexuality is God's gift to you. You must protect it and fight for its purity! Ezekiel 23:3 says, *"They committed harlotry in their youth; their breasts were there embraced, their virgin bosom was there pressed."* Ephesians 5:3 emphasizes that believers should not even allow a hint of sexual immorality to plague their lives.

> **Sexuality is God's gift to you. You must protect it and fight for its purity!**

Even though premarital sex is not a biblical option for Christian singles, some resort to skirting the rules—heavy petting, making out, vulgar dancing, fondling, and having sex with the clothes on. You are progressing in the wrong direction. What do you expect the end result to be? There is no need to frustrate yourselves sexually. Don't even go there!

Unfortunately, our society often holds a double standard that says boys will be boys, and that girls must discern sexual temptations. The following is a list of the seven lines that boys typically say to girls to pressure them to engage in sexual activity before marriage:

1. "If you really loved me, you would."
2. "Everybody's doing it."
3. "I'm so excited, I can't stop."
4. "You will not get pregnant."
5. "If you get pregnant, I will marry you."
6. "We're going to get married anyway."
7. "Nobody will ever know about it."

If Satan can persuade young women into believing just one of these lies, then he has robbed them of their purity and sexual integrity. We must teach our daughters to preserve and guard their virginity. We must teach our sons to respect sex as a sacred thing that is reserved for marriage. Statistics show that 42 percent of teens, ages 13–17, see having a baby outside of marriage as morally acceptable.[2] If we don't instill into our sons and daughters the beauty and sanctity of sex within marriage, who will? The pressure to go along with the crowd is greater than ever. The need to fit in and be liked at any price will cause you to live a life of regret.

> It's easy to compromise in little ways, but they are more harmful than they seem.

Even though we live in a hostile environment externally, we must constantly renew our minds in God's Word and guard our hearts from evil. It's easy to compromise in little ways that, in reality, are more harmful than they seem.

There is nothing wrong with having fun or wanting to be attractive to the opposite sex, but you must learn to protect yourself from destructive relationships that are born out of lust.

BEWARE OF SEXUAL SIGNALS

Ladies, one of the areas you must avoid is wearing suggestive clothing. The weakness of every man is a woman's body. When putting your clothes on, you know exactly what kind of reaction and effect it will have on men. With food, it has been

---

[2] Linda Lyons, *Teens' Marriage Views Reflect Changing Norms*, The Gallup Organization, November 18, 2003.

said that presentation is everything; the same is true for the body. Dressing fashionably and attractively is different from dressing in a way that flaunts your body as if you are sending out a sexual invitation. Things have certainly changed from a few years ago. Now, it is not unusual to see a Christian woman strolling down the street wearing a short shirt and low-rise jeans just to show off her belly button ring.

The way you dress teaches people how to treat you. You teach the opposite sex to respect you or to disrespect you by the attire you wear. First Timothy 2:9–10 teaches women to *"adorn themselves in modest apparel, with propriety and moderation...but, which is proper for women professing godliness, with good works."* If that voice on the inside whispers, *This neckline is too low, That skirt is too short,* or *Those jeans are too tight,* you should listen. Let the redeemed of the Lord dress so, not just say so!

And, men, don't allow your eye to be the gateway to the lusts of the flesh. It's impossible to avoid being exposed to all the temptations out there, but you can stay away from situations that may cause you problems. Be aware of the TV you watch and the Internet sites you view. Protect your mind from access to improper images. Premarital sex only appears to be free of strings attached. But, in reality, it leads to addiction, sexually transmitted diseases, unwanted pregnancies, marital problems, and infidelity.

The cost of running sexual red lights is very high. You must balance the outward power of the world's hostilities with an inward thrust of moral conviction and dedication. First Thessalonians 4:3 says, *"For this is the will of God, your sanctification: that you should abstain from sexual immorality."* The word *abstain* means "to willfully hold back."

You can measure what kind of Christian you are by the cost you are willing to pay. What is your Christian life costing you? It costs something to dress modestly. It costs something to monitor the TV shows, movies, and music you listen to. It costs something to miss out on all the so-called fun that everyone else is having because what they're doing violates your code of ethics. It costs something to decide not to be popular with the opposite sex for all the wrong reasons.

> You can measure the kind of Christian you are by the cost you're willing to pay.

We live in a society where anything goes. I want to ask you a question. Do you find yourself doing things you feel the need to hide? (See 1 John 1:6.) If you're hiding things from your parents, things like steamy love notes, books, or movies that you would be embarrassed to talk about at church, then you are stepping into the darkness to do things you're ashamed of in the light.

GOD REDEEMS AND RESTORES

Maybe you already feel like damaged goods because of things you have done in your past. You feel that no respectable man or woman of God would want you. You may feel as though you have to give men what they want, or nobody will want to date or marry you. You may have given in to temptation and now you don't know how a "pure" girl will accept you.

I assure you that God has destined someone to love you. Rest assured that he or she is living and breathing right now somewhere on this planet. He or she is going to love God and love you passionately. Your job is to trust God and from this

174

day forward keep yourself just for that special someone God will send to you.

God is a matchmaker! When He ties the knot in a relationship, it will hold—if you don't pick at the knot. Ecclesiastes 4:12 says that a threefold cord is not easily broken. You can't afford to have a twofold cord, which is a relationship committed just to each other. You must have a threefold cord relationship: you, your mate, and God intertwined together in a loving relationship.

According to the Bible, *"there are eunuchs who have made themselves eunuchs for the kingdom of heaven's sake"* (Matthew 19:12). To be a eunuch is to be sexually inactive. You can approach your sexually inactive single years in one of three ways: you can be a griper, a grabber, or a gripper.

Do you gripe all the time because you're not married or, depending upon your age, because you're not dating as much as you think you should?

Or are you a grabber? You will grab hold of anyone you can date or marry, regardless of reputation. You're like the old maid who was praying under a tree asking God for a husband, when she heard an owl in the tree saying, "Whooooo, whoooo!" She replied, "Anybody, Lord. Anybody will do!"

Anybody won't do! Don't be a griper or a grabber—be a gripper. This is someone who firmly grips hold of God's purpose. God said that it was not good for man to be alone, so, most likely, it is His will for you to marry. You may ask, "What about Paul?" He was single, yes, but unless you've given yourself so fully to God's work that you have no desire to be married, then God has someone for you when the time is right. You may not understand now, but God's timing is perfect.

175

To the man or woman contemplating marriage, I would ask, "What are your dreams? What goals have you set for yourself that you want to achieve before marriage?" You need a firm grip on God's purpose for your life. You need to use this time of waiting as a time of preparation. If you are half a person, you will attract half a mate. Quit attracting halves and start attracting wholes. It's all about His timing! Use this time alone to grip hold of God's plan for your life. Do you have emotional baggage you need to unload? Do you have your finances in order? Take advantage of this time to prepare yourself for marriage.

> If you wait on God and remain pure, He will bring you a mate when the time is right.

Note two things about the first marriage in Genesis. First, God knew what kind of mate Adam needed; and second, it was God who brought Eve to Adam. It is not unrealistic to believe that if you will wait on God and be sexually pure, then He will bring the right mate to you when the time is right. Don't waste valuable time until then.

Several years ago, I spoke to 24,000 teenagers in Knoxville, Tennessee. The message I preached became one of my most requested. It was entitled, "Keep Your Underwear On!" Exodus 28:42–43 tells us about what the high priests who came into God's presence were to wear: *You shall make for them linen trousers to cover their nakedness; they shall reach from the waist to the thighs"* (verse 42). Beneath the white robe, the priest was commanded to have "his underwear on." No matter how religious the priest looked outwardly in his priestly robe, if beneath his religious garb he did not have his linen britches on, then God would not allow him to live in His presence. (See Exodus 28:43.) In essence, the priest had to have sexual integrity in his private life.

Outwardly, many people have perfected their religious image. They look one way on the outside, but, in private, they are someone else. First Samuel teaches, *"Man looks at the outward appearance, but the LORD looks at the heart"* (1 Samuel 16:7). If you want to live in the presence of God and have His favor on your life, then you must "Keep Your Underwear On!"

I waited until I was twenty-five to get married. I was a virgin, and my wife was a virgin. Don't believe the deceptive lie of Satan when he tells you that it is not possible to remain sexually pure until marriage. We were both virgins. Today we have five children, so obviously we have made up for all those years of abstinence!

> There are intimacies reserved for friendship, courtship, and some only for marriage.

When Cherise and I started dating, it wasn't long until we began to fulfill the Scripture, *"Greet one another with a holy kiss"* (Romans 16:16). It became our favorite verse. As our relationship progressed, we fell deeply in love. After we were engaged, we felt we needed to fulfill another Scripture as soon as possible: *"It is better to marry than to burn with passion"* (1 Corinthians 7:9). We even moved up the wedding date.

Naturally, as you begin to date, the relationship develops and there will be different intimacies reserved for each stage of the relationship. Understand that there are some intimacies reserved for friendship, others for courtship, and others only for engagement. Of course sexual intercourse is reserved for the confines of marriage only.

I realize you are not going to walk up to someone and say, "Hi, Bob, I'm Jean. Let's get married in six months. I'll see you at the altar." First, you go through a growing and bonding process. What you must guard against is allowing a level of intimacy that is not sexually legitimate to cross over into relationships where they do not belong.

First Thessalonians 4:3–6 says,

For this is the will of God, your sanctification: that you should abstain from sexual immorality; that each of you should know how to possess his own vessel in sanctification and honor, not in passion of lust, like the Gentiles who do not know God; that no one should take advantage of and defraud his brother [or sister] *in this matter.*

Paul was saying that you should not arouse sexual desires in another person that you cannot righteously satisfy. I know that when you love someone and plan to marry and spend the rest of your life together, it is hard to walk away when the desire for each other is so strong. But trust me, it can be done.

Why should you maintain your sexual purity?

1. *So you won't shame the name of Jesus.*

Samson fell to sexual sin, and the Philistines made sport of his God. (See Judges 16:23–25.) When we compromise our sexual integrity, we drag the sacred name of Jesus through the mud. We've all seen this happen, particularly when moral failure is exposed in the clergy.

2. *So your witness won't be discredited.*

This sin cripples your testimony to all the people to whom you have witnessed. It will discredit your witness because what you were offering did not work.

3. *So you won't contract sexually transmitted diseases.*

Today, not only are preachers preaching abstinence, but doctors and health experts are warning that multiple sexual partners can cost you your life—or that of your loved one!

If at any point you discern an alarm going off in your spirit saying, *Warning! This isn't right,* you had better listen to it. God put that radar there. You may have ignored it in the past, but from now on, you should listen to it.

Don't repeatedly ignore the voice of discernment inside of you, or you may become desensitized to real danger. Remember, nobody can guard your body and your sexual purity but you. Defending your virginity is your responsibility.

I want to drive home the fact that if you are single and sexually inactive, you are not a freak! If you will be God's best, He will send you His best!

How many times have you read those infamous headlines at the supermarket checkout lines? "Learn to Please Your Man!" "Lose Weight in Ten Days!" "Be Happy!" On and on, the media plays on "surefire" ways to help women become happier, stronger, and more successful in life. Millions of dollars are spent on advertisements geared specifically for women who feel less than adequate in one or more areas of their lives. I don't have a problem with magazines promoting good health or lifestyle improvements for women; I just hate the fact that so many women are not finding out the truth about who they are and what they possess.

Beauty is good, and much appreciated by men. I thank God that I have a beautiful wife; but, more importantly, I thank God that I have a discerning wife. Real beauty comes from within, just as real happiness comes from within. Proverbs

31:10 asks the question, *"Who can find a virtuous wife? For her worth is far above rubies."* Her husband can safely trust in her. She will do him good and not evil all the days of her life. (See Proverbs 31:11–12.)

Ladies, in order for you to achieve all the things you desire—beauty, health, happiness, success, and good relationships—you must know the truth about how to achieve these things. It is not by achieving the ultimate dress size or learning how to please a man. No, the way to achieve all you desire is to become the woman God created you to be. Focus on pleasing Him.

Men, what is on the inside is far more important than what is on the outside. Beauty is vain; it will fade away, but the inner beauty of a discerning woman will live on. She will leave a legacy long after she is gone. *"Her children rise up and call her blessed; her husband also, and he praises her....Charm is deceitful and beauty is passing, but a woman who fears the LORD, she shall be praised"* (Proverbs 31:28, 30).

Chapter Fourteen

DISCERNMENT TO WIN YOUR FAMILY

Believe on the Lord Jesus Christ,
and you will be saved, you and your household.
—Acts 16:31

Have you ever noticed there are more women in the church than men? More and more, women are finding it necessary to become the spiritual leaders of their homes. More often than not, it is the wife who first encounters God; then, hopefully, the husband follows in her spiritual footsteps. It is the rare case when the husband is on fire for God and the wife elects to stay at home.

What do you do when you have an experience with God before your mate does?

In Judges 13, we read about a case of marital, parental, and spiritual incompatibility. Samson's father, Manoah, was a passive, laid-back, low-key person. The name *Manoah* actually means "rest." There is nothing wrong with a mild-mannered man who has a calm temperament. However, this Scripture indicates that he was also low-key and laid-back concerning spiritual things.

Manoah's wife is one of the nameless women in the Old Testament. All we are told about her is that she was barren and remained childless for a long period of time until an angel of the Lord appeared, not to Manoah, but to her. God informed her that she would have a child and instructed her to raise the child observing the Nazarite vow—a disciplined life with strict rules of diet and hygiene. (See Judges 13:3–4.)

It is significant that the angel appeared, not to Manoah, but to his wife. The angel informed her directly rather than going through her husband.

How should a woman handle it when God speaks to her first? What do you do when your man is laid-back and low-key about spiritual things and you are not? What do you do when you are excited about Jesus, the church, and the Word of God, but he seldom wants to go to church or discuss spiritual matters? It's tough when you come home from church excited about what the Lord is doing in your life, while your husband is snoring on the couch, or out hunting, or watching sports on TV.

Spiritual incompatibility is a real problem for many couples. It affects the relationship on all levels. It is a great area of testing for many marriages, and it takes a wise woman to know how to handle this challenge.

INCITE SPIRITUAL JEALOUSY

Manoah's wife is a perfect example of a woman whose marriage was incompatible on several different levels. She had a spiritual encounter with God before her husband did. Then the angel of the Lord gave her specific instructions about how to raise her son, Samson. Manoah and his wife experienced parental and spiritual incompatibility.

Samson was to be raised a Nazarite. The Nazarite vow was an act of consecration. The person taking this vow was to avoid anything from the vine (no wine), could not touch anything that was dead, and was not to cut his hair until the resolution of the vow. This child was to be separated and isolated for God's use. He would live a restricted lifestyle that would require great discipline. In order to raise a child according to the Nazarite vow, the father and mother both had to be extremely committed. As sure as Manoah's wife was of what God was telling them, Manoah was left in the dark. (See Judges 13:2–24.)

How do you raise kids to live for God when their father doesn't live for God? This woman would have a son whom she wanted to set apart for God's call, but the father was oblivious to God's will.

Instead of acting independently or maneuvering to get her husband to do what was required, she was patient with her husband until Manoah finally prayed a powerful prayer:

O my Lord, please let the Man of God whom You sent come to us again and teach us what we shall do for the child who will be born. (Judges 13:8)

How do you raise your kids to live for God when only one of the parents is a believer? Manoah's wife gives us a fine example. She wasn't ugly to her husband; she didn't move out of their bedroom because he didn't share her faith. She didn't badger her husband, or compare him to "So-and-so's" husband, who was so spiritual. She simply communicated what God had said to her and, as hard as it must have been, waited for God to speak to him.

What makes you think God can't speak to your spouse? I don't care if he has cotton in his ears. I don't care if he gets drunk or high, God can speak to him.

Let me encourage you to pray this prayer:

God, I know he's not spiritual right now, but speak to him. He needs to know how to raise our children, so speak to him. God, as the priest of our home, I need him to cover me spiritually. Speak to him on the job or in his sleep. Speak to him in his car or in the shower. Speak to him through circumstances and through other people. But please speak to him!

Manoah's wife had an awesome revelation about how God wanted to use her son, but her husband was out of the loop. When she told him what the angel had told her, he wanted to have the same experience she had. There was something about this woman that provoked her husband to spiritual jealousy. She didn't provoke him to anger, nor did her encounter with God provoke him to frustration. If she were always moaning and complaining and wore her discontent on her sleeve, why would Manoah

> She lived out her faith and it provoked her husband to crave what she had.

have wanted any part of that? Instead, she lived out her faith in such a way that it provoked her husband to spiritual jealousy—he craved what she had.

Spiritual jealousy, inspired by the life his discerning wife modeled before him, lit a fire in Manoah for the same spiritual relationship with God that his wife enjoyed. Live your life so that your husband will want what you have. Let him observe how gently you have treated him, when you could have embarrassed him or cut him down. A holy life will produce the deepest impressions.

In 1 Corinthians 7, Paul had advice for the lone believing spouse:

> *But to the rest I, not the Lord, say: if any brother has a wife who does not believe, and she is willing to live with him, let him not divorce her. And a woman who has a husband who does not believe, if he is willing to live with her, let her not divorce him. For the unbelieving husband is sanctified by the wife, and the unbelieving wife is sanctified by the husband....But if the unbeliever departs, let him depart; a brother or a sister is not under bondage in such cases. But God has called us to peace. For how do you know, O wife, whether you will save your husband? Or how do you know, O husband, whether you will save your wife?*
>
> (verses 12–16)

Live your life in such a way that your husband will:

- Feel the warmth of your sweet spirit
- See the joy of the Lord in your life
- Feel loved as you pour respect and honor into him

MARRYING THE ILLUSION

The real world of marriage is not always peaches and cream. The problem is that we marry illusions. It seems God has a sense of humor because He doesn't always give us the illusion we wanted. For example, you looked at that man before you were married and you envisioned him attending church with you, holding the Bible in his hands, and leading the kids in devotions at night—so wonderful and spiritual and sensitive.

But after the honeymoon, the only time he goes to church with you is when someone is *hatched* (baby dedication), *matched* (wedding), or *dispatched* (funeral). He's a CEO Christian—Christmas and Easter only.

Men can marry illusions as well. You imagine coming home from work to the sight of your beautiful wife waiting at the front door with your bedroom slippers and silk robe.

She asks, "How was your day, darling?"

You answer, "It was torture."

Then she says, "Kiss me, you fool," as you fall into one another's arms and begin to rip off each other's clothes.

> You must reach beyond romance to responsibility, beyond sex to sensitivity.

Nice fantasy; but it's not real life.

Another illusion is the physical illusion. They say love is blind, so you don't see any of the physical flaws while you are dating. But a few years after you are married, you begin to notice all of his physical imperfections. His belly is hanging over his belt, he burps after meals, and he snores in bed. Or, your once perfect, swimsuit-model wife has packed on some pounds, she doesn't always wear makeup and do her hair, and she snores something awful as well!

You stare at the person lying next to you and wonder, *What did I marry?*

After the violins stop playing, and the bubbles have burst in the heart-shaped Jacuzzi, sometimes you feel real pain the next morning. Your marriage will not always pan out like the soap opera *Days of Our Lives*. These are the "days of your life," when you must reach beyond romance to responsibility, beyond sex to sensitivity. This is where the highway can become littered with casualties who signed up for marriage without fully realizing what they were signing up for.

You didn't marry a Hollywood star. This is a real man or woman, from the crown of his or her head to the soles of his or her feet. Maybe he's no Prince Charming. Maybe she's no Sleeping Beauty. He might not be as spiritual or as romantic as you wish, but he's yours! She may not be your mother in the kitchen or your fantasy in the bedroom, but she's yours! If you don't want to face the devastation of divorce, you need to make it work.

> **If you don't want to face the devastation of divorce, you need to make your marriage work.**

Ladies, there are not many good men around—you better concentrate on what you have! You can't read *Esquire* and *Cosmopolitan* and win this battle. Oprah can't tell you how to have a successful marriage because she's never been married herself.

Gentlemen, there probably isn't a long line of women just waiting to grace you with their presence. Appreciate the one who is there on the sidelines, cheering you on.

Ladies, there are some things you just should not do in public. I don't care how ADD he is, I don't care if he's got his entire foot in his mouth, don't embarrass and belittle him publicly. If he gets his words mixed up, if he makes a mistake, stand right there by his side and grin as though he could do no wrong. Afterwards, in the privacy of your home or car, you can discuss it if you feel the need.

Gentlemen, your wife is a reflection of you. Her countenance will be a reflection of how you treat her. Treat her with disrespect, contempt, and shame, and that is how she will appear. Treasure her as your queen, and your queen she shall be. You can't mistreat her at home and expect her to shine in public. She's not that good an actor.

DISCERNING INTIMACY

Some think that being a Christian means that we have to be offended at anything sexual. Many unsaved men resent the church because it turns their wives into a holier-than-thou "church lady." Before they were saved, the marriage and sex were great. She wore pink lingerie to bed, and sex was wonderfully creative! But now that she's born again, she wears a granny gown and sleeps with a Bible lying on her bosom. Whenever he makes advances toward her, she says, in a religious, stained-glass voice, "Touch not God's anointed."

That may be a humorous image, but when it's time to be intimate in your marriage, if you're lying in bed speaking in tongues, he's wondering, *What has that church done to my wife?*

Make him jealous of your spirituality, not resentful of it. For too long, the church has been a haven for disgruntled women whose lives are out of balance. God created sex for marriage.

Married couples learn how to please each other; singles learn how to please the Lord. If you are married, a major part of pleasing the Lord is in your ministry to your spouse.

Scripture says, *"Do not deprive one another except with consent for a time, that you may give yourselves to fasting and prayer; and come together again so that Satan does not tempt you because of your lack of self-control"* (1 Corinthians 7:5). That means that the sexual relationship in a marriage should be so frequent that you only refrain from sex for a short time of fasting and prayer. Then, as soon as the fast is complete, you get back to business! Consistency is important; don't give Satan an opportunity to tempt you with unfaithfulness.

YOUR MARRIAGE ASSIGNMENT

When you and your spouse are spiritually incompatible, it's easy to become frustrated and build up bitterness and resentment. If you will roll into his arms instead of rolling toward the wall, or if you will cook him his favorite meal when he least deserves it, then you are planting seeds into his heart that will cause him to want what you've got spiritually. Manoah's wife decided to make her marriage work even though she and her husband were spiritually incompatible.

What she desired was for God to show her husband their assignment—His eternal purpose for this couple being together. God wanted them to raise Samson as the champion who would deliver God's people.

Every marriage has an assignment. God didn't put you together just to have sex, a house payment, and a two-car garage. When you enter the kingdom of God, you receive an assignment. Your children have a divine assignment, and the enemy wants to abort it. That's why divorce is so devastating; it not only affects the husband and the wife, but it destroys God's assignment for the entire family.

It's hard to come home to an unspiritual man. It's hard to raise your children according to God's Word when your mate is not saved. Manoah's wife shows us that when you're living with a man who is not spiritual, you can provoke him to spiritual hunger.

Finally, the angel of the Lord appeared to Manoah, too. After this visitation, he went to his wife and asked for further instructions. If your mate is unsaved, don't talk to him about spiritual things all the time. Sometimes discernment means being quiet until God gives you the opportunity to speak. At the right time, God will give you a chance to talk.

> Sometimes discernment means being quiet until God tells you to speak.

When that door opens, ease on in. *"The wise woman builds her house, but the foolish pulls it down with her hands"* (Proverbs 14:1).

Psalm 68:6 says, *"God setteth the solitary in families: he bringeth out those which are bound with chains"* (KJV). The word *solitary* means "single," in reference to a single diamond, a precious jewel. In other words, I believe God hovers over families, and He finds one single, solitary diamond in every family. He sovereignly picks one member of the family to deliver those bound with spiritual chains.

Do you know why God saved you first? You are His beachhead—God's entry point, God's doorway—through which He will reach the rest of your family.

Manoah and his wife raised Samson. They fulfilled the assignment of God upon their family. Samson grew up and became a mighty deliverer of God's people.

Over ten years ago, my personal assistant, Susan, was the first and only member of her family to be born again. For two years, she attended church alone. Every Sunday after church, she went home to her husband and her twenty-year-old son, who did not share her faith. Her husband, Alan, was a good man and a good provider. He just was not interested in spiritual things. Sunday was his day to drink beer and play golf.

Often, Susan would leave the atmosphere of praise and worship at church and go home to her husband and son who were totally unspiritual. Many nights she cried herself to sleep, wondering if her family would ever be saved and share her faith.

After two years of coming to church by herself and living for God alone in their home, the Holy Spirit began to speak to her about how to win her husband. He challenged her to control her tongue. As she began to show Alan respect, honor, and unconditional love, slowly his heart began to melt.

She prayed Ephesians 1:17–18 for him every day:

That the God of our Lord Jesus Christ, the Father of glory, may give to you the spirit of wisdom and revelation in the knowledge of Him, the eyes of your understanding being enlightened; that you may know what is the hope of His calling, what are the riches of the glory of His inheritance in the saints.

She was winning him without a word. Her gentle, kind spirit was witnessing to him.

As Alan watched the change in his wife, he started attending church with her one September. Even though he was not converted immediately, every Sunday he attended church with Susan.

Tracy, their twenty-year-old son, observed his father going to church week after week with his mother. By early October, Tracy decided to check out church. That Sunday morning, Tracy walked down the aisle, was born again, and was filled with the Holy Spirit.

A few weeks later, at the end of October, I preached an illustrated sermon, where Tracy played one of the characters. When I gave the altar call that morning, Alan walked down the aisle and was gloriously saved and filled with the Holy Spirit.

God had an awesome assignment for this family. Tracy began to exhibit extraordinary leadership gifts. Several years later, he became the children's pastor in our church. Today, he ministers to over a thousand kids a week. He also has been instrumental in helping me reach tens of thousands of teenagers by assisting me with illustrated sermons.

Over the years, Satan had tried to convince Susan that her family would never be saved, but this discerning woman kept on praying and loving. She was patient and kind to her husband. She knew God had an assignment for her family, and she would not give up until God brought it to pass.

Today, she is in full-time ministry as my personal assistant. Her son, Tracy, is in full-time ministry as children's pastor of Free Chapel. Her husband, Alan, is one of the greatest Christians I know. What if Susan had given up?

What assignment will you abort if you give up on your family? Acts 16:31 says, *"Believe on the Lord Jesus Christ, and you will be saved, you and your household."*

God has set you as a solitary diamond in your family to deliver those bound with chains. Like Manoah's wife, you are going to see God's assignment for your family come to pass.

Chapter Fifteen

A LIFE WORTH REMEMBERING

She has done what she could....Assuredly, I say to you,
wherever this gospel is preached in the whole world,
what this woman has done will also
be told as a memorial to her.

—Mark 14:8–9

Ask yourself, A hundred years from now, will it even matter that I was born? Are the things I'm living for worth Christ's dying for?

In the *Guinness Book of World Records*, I read about a man who eats glass, metal, and wood. He has eaten ten bicycles, a supermarket cart, and seven television sets. But the most astonishing reason he will forever be remembered is that he ate a Cessna light-flying aircraft, after grinding it up and mixing it with his food. That's how this man attained his "fifteen minutes of fame."

Imagine him standing before God one day. The Lord asks him, in a baritone voice, "What did you do with your life?"

His only answer, "I ate an airplane!"

How will you be remembered? What kind of legacy are you leaving for your family?

WHAT CAN YOU DO?

The Gospels tell of a woman who lived a life worth remembering. Jesus was dining at the home of Simon the leper when a woman approached with an alabaster jar of costly perfume. She broke the jar and poured the perfume on Jesus' head and feet. Lovingly, she wiped the perfume from His feet with her hair, weeping as she did so. Jesus, aware of what was to come, accepted it as His anointment for burial. (See Matthew 26:6–13; Mark 14:3–9; Luke 7:36–48.)

Others who were present, including the disciples, were bothered by this. Some questioned the waste of expensive perfume when it could have been sold and the money given to the poor.

In Luke, it says that she *"stood at His feet behind Him weeping; and she began to wash His feet with her tears, and wiped them with the hair of her head; and she kissed His feet and anointed them with the fragrant oil"* (Luke 7:38). In that one verse is a list of five things that she did for Jesus, and they all regard His feet.

- She stood at the feet of Jesus.
- She washed the feet of Jesus.
- She dried His feet with her hair.
- She kissed His feet.
- She anointed His feet.

Jesus was so moved by this woman's passionate worship that He forever immortalized her. *"Wherever this gospel is preached in the whole world, what this woman has done will also be told as a memorial to her"* (Mark 14:9).

194

Her life became memorable not for the things that she couldn't do, but for the fact that *"she* [did] *what she could"* (Mark 14:8). God will never ask you to do what you can't do. If He asks you for something, it just means He's already put in you the ability to do what He's asking. Don't insult God by telling Him you can't do it.

> **God will never ask you to do what you can't do.**

This woman not only did what she could, but she also did it in the face of criticism. Jesus' host for the evening, a Pharisee, said, *"This man, if He were a prophet, would know who and what manner of woman this is who is touching Him, for she is a sinner"* (Luke 7:39).

Imagine her shame and embarrassment as, while she was washing Jesus' feet, others in the room called her a sinner. This was not news to her. She knew that. Isn't it amazing how many people will criticize you when you start to do something for Jesus? Her critics attacked her. They accused, "What you're doing is a waste." Still, she did what she could.

STRENGTH IN BROKENNESS

In the 1950s, Paul Anderson was the strongest man in the world. He was able to carry 6,270 pounds on his back.

Once he was asked, "Were you ever a ninety-pound weakling?

He replied, "Yes, when I was four years old."

One day at church, Paul was moved to give his life to Christ while hearing a quadriplegic man give his testimony.

How about that? The strongest man in the world was won to Christ by one considered to be among the weakest. God used the weakest man He could find who was willing to do what he could do.

For God to use you, you will have to pass the praise test and the criticism test. How do you pass these tests? You learn to give the praise and criticism you've received to God. Jesus immortalized this woman because of her extravagant worship. He was moved when she broke open the alabaster jar of expensive oil to anoint His head and feet.

"We have this treasure in earthen vessels" (2 Corinthians 4:7). You and I are the earthen vessels, and the treasure on the inside is our worship to God. If people are going to know about your love for Him, there must be brokenness. Just as the alabaster box was broken, we too must be broken in order to offer Him praise. Many people will never live a life worth remembering because they are not willing to be broken—they want to strut. You don't have to be a superachiever or have a great IQ. You don't have to be amazingly talented. All you have to do to be used by God is be broken enough to pour out your love on Jesus. If, in doing so, you get an inroad to win one soul, then you will have lived a life worth remembering for all eternity in God's eyes.

I want to salute some men and women who are living lives worth remembering.

1. I salute the fathers and mothers who stick with their children through thick and thin.

In John 18:25, the most famous mother in the world was standing at the foot of the cross, while her precious Son was being crucified.

In the midst of dying, Jesus tenderly instructed John the beloved to take care of His mother. Mary was present when He was born, and she was present when He died. She was there to console her Son in His darkest hour. Men try to act grown, but if they get in real trouble, they want their mother's comfort. Jesus was no different. In His hour of trouble, He wanted His mother near. It had to be very difficult for Mary to see her Son precede her in death.

Often, people are who they are because they had praying parents or grandparents in their lives. Some of you reading this book have parents who chose to have you instead of pursuing great personal success. They could have gone to college themselves, but they paid your tuition. They could have retired by now or could be living a better lifestyle, but they made some tremendous sacrifices to help you do things they've never done or go places they've never been. Children don't always appreciate the enormous sacrifices their parents have made to ensure a better way of life for them. I want to commend every mother and father who has stood by their children in the good times and the bad times.

I want to warn you not to love your children to death. Sometimes we can love our children so much that we are practicing borderline idolatry. You have to discern when you are loving your child to death instead of loving your child to life. When you let them talk to you disrespectfully without disciplining them, you love them to death, instead of loving them to life. Some people don't prepare their children for the harsh realities of the real world. When we don't show our children tough love at times when discipline is necessary, we can actually be sowing seeds of rebellion into them that make them think rules don't apply to them.

You can go overboard in sacrificing yourself for your kids. When you love them to the point where you don't want anyone else to spend time with them, you're going overboard with your love. When you feel nobody is good enough to marry them or date them because you're so picky, your obsession with your children is hurting them, not helping them.

Love your children, support your children, and stand by your children, like Mary did on her Son's toughest day as He went to the cross. Never give up on your kids. Love them to life, not to death.

2. I salute mothers, fathers, and children in nontraditional families.

I also want to salute the mother who did what was best for her child, even if it meant giving him up for adoption. Not everyone will have agreed with your decision, but at least you had the courage to birth the child rather than abort him. It took courage to release the child into a loving, stable family.

Moses' mother hid him for three months because of Pharaoh's decree to kill all male children two years old or younger. I'm sure it was a difficult decision to send her crying infant down the Nile River in a basket. She was forced to give up her baby. Adoption is a very sensitive issue. Millions of women have had to give up their children by force or by choice, trying to do what is best for their children.

As teenage pregnancies continue to rise, some high schools are designated only for children who are pregnant. When I was growing up, if a girl became pregnant, her academic career was pretty much over. She was forced to drop out of school.

Today, the family is being redefined. Millions of children are living in homes that don't fit the stereotype of what a traditional family is supposed to be.

Just because you're a single-parent family doesn't mean your family can't function well in the sight of God. On the other hand, just because you have a perfect home setting with a two-parent family does not mean you have a wonderful home life.

The ideal family setting is two parents: mom and dad raising their children together. I remember reading in the Bible about a traditional family that had two parents. The mother was a homemaker, the father was a farmer, working by the sweat of his brow, and they had two children. They had everything their hearts desired; they didn't want for anything. Nevertheless, they ended up homeless. And in a domestic violence dispute, one of the sons killed his brother.

Don't allow family pain or shame to hold you hostage to the past.

The parents were Adam and Eve, and their sons were Cain and Abel. According to the standards of the world, they were the perfect family, living in the perfect environment. Yet they still became a very dysfunctional family.

Don't allow family pain or shame to hold you hostage to the past. Moses' mother had to give her child up, not because she didn't love him, but to save his life! Maybe you were raised by one parent, a grandmother, or some other relative. Maybe you were given up for adoption. As a result, feelings of worthlessness may flood your emotions. Why would my mother or father give me up? Perhaps, like Moses' mother, yours did what she had to do to save your life.

Moses' mother did what was best for her son. She knew that, under her present conditions, she couldn't give him what he needed. Pharaoh's daughter eventually adopted Moses. He lived in somebody else's house, not with his real mother. However, he lived a better life than he would have if his natural mother had raised him. Thank God for people who take children into their homes and invest in their lives by loving and treating the children as one of their very own. You're living a life worth remembering.

3. I salute every single parent who has raised children alone.

In 1 Kings 17, we read the story of a widow and her child living in the midst of a famine. This single-parent home was on a strict budget. Mother and child were down to their last meal.

Perhaps you have had to make tremendous sacrifices working two jobs or more, just to make ends meet while raising children all by yourself. You tried to do what was right in front of your children, doing it alone. Congress can't seem to balance the budget in Washington, D.C. Perhaps they need to take lessons from the amazing single parents who live on a shoestring budget with kids to feed and clothe.

I salute you. You're living a life worth remembering.

In 1 Kings 17, the poor widow opened her house to the prophet Elijah. When he asked her to share some food from her meager rations, she explained her dire circumstances. Elijah then demonstrated the abundant resources of God for single parents who show faith:

And Elijah said to her, "Do not fear; go and do as you have said, but make me a small cake from it first, and bring it to me; and afterward make some for yourself and your son. For thus says the LORD God of Israel: 'The bin of flour shall not be used up, nor shall the jar of oil run dry, until the day the LORD sends rain on the earth.'" So she went away and did according to the word of Elijah; and she and he and her household ate for many days. (1 Kings 17:13–15)

I want to salute the mothers who have been pushed out of the way. It is a hard pill to swallow, but it happens every day. When a man divorces his wife and leaves his kids from his first marriage, that doesn't make them just go away. Just because a man gets a new wife and a new family doesn't mean the old family doesn't exist.

Many of you may be in a similar situation. Somebody closed the book on you and rode off into the sunset. He can't do enough for his new family, but he has totally forgotten about you and your children. We're living in a society where it has become normal for people to get divorced and then move on like nothing ever happened. Men can get a woman pregnant and then just ride off into the sunset to become successful.

God, however, stands ready to protect you. If you will not become bitter, He will bless you and your children. I have a word from the Lord for you: Even if the child's father never blesses you, God will bless you! Lift your head up. Don't let anybody make you feel ashamed. If you won't get bitter, God will be *"a father of the fatherless, a defender of widows"* (Psalm 68:5).

4. I salute grandparents who are raising the children of their children.

I want to salute those of you who may not have given birth yourself to the kids you are raising, but you've taken someone else's children, perhaps your son's or daughter's.

It is estimated that over six million grandparents are raising their grandchildren as their own. Sometimes, because of their children's addictions or immoral lifestyles, grandparents with big hearts are opening up their homes and adopting their grandchildren. They are living a life of sacrifice by investing in the lives of their grandchildren as if the children were their own.

Just like the woman whom Jesus immortalized in Scripture, yours is also a life worth remembering.

DISCERNING THE PRESENCE OF THE SPIRIT OF JESUS

In Luke 2, Mary, Joseph, and their twelve-year-old Son, Jesus, had been in Jerusalem for the Feast of the Passover. Religious activity had filled their days. Crammed full of what had happened in the temple, they started their long trek home.

A day into their journey home, they noticed that Jesus was missing. Mary and Joseph frantically checked with all of the relatives in their party, but Jesus was not to be found.

Here's the lesson in the story of lost Jesus. Immediately after having such a tremendous spiritual feast, Mary and Joseph lost the presence of Jesus. Even as they traveled in a caravan with all their religious friends and relatives, who had joined them in their religious exercise, they still lost the personal presence of Jesus!

If there is one thing I want you to carry with you after reading this book, even if you forget everything else, it is this: you must be very discerning so as not to lose the personal presence of the Spirit of Jesus! You cannot take Him for granted.

When you're not in the temple, ask yourself, *Do I have His personal presence? Am I fellowshipping with Him and taking Him into my home?*

Mary and Joseph had Jesus with them in the temple. They lost Him on the way home. Jesus doesn't just want to be with you in church. He wants you to take Him into your home, and into your daily life.

Don't start for home and lose the personal presence of Jesus. The most unlikely person to lose Jesus was Mary, His mother. I question if anybody loved and understood Him as much as Mary did. She was in His inner circle, but Mary lost Him. How close she was to Jesus! Their very lives were interwoven together. He was part of her; she was part of Him. Yet she lost Him. Although you may get very close to Jesus, you must be very careful that you do not then lose Him.

Not only did Mary lose Him, she didn't even recognize it. The Scripture said, *"Supposing Him to have been in the company"* (Luke 2:44). She thought He was there. Isn't that the danger with all of us? We take too much for granted. We don't do that in our businesses. We take nothing for granted, closely examining the books and balance sheets. But when it comes to our relationship with Christ, we get comfortable with merely assuming that He is in our company.

Notice again that Mary and Joseph were among religious people when they lost Christ. Not only was Mary the most unlikely person to lose Him, not only did she lose Him and not know it, but she also lost Him in the most unusual place. Where? Not at a theatre, casino, or club; she lost Him in the temple among holy things, among holy surroundings.

Mary and Joseph lived three days without Him. When they finally found Jesus, they found Him where they had lost Him, in the temple. At first they blamed Him, but Jesus reminded them that He was in His Father's house—the temple—where they had left Him.

Where did the prodigal son find his father? Exactly where he had left him!

You'll find Jesus where you lost Him. If you'll only go back there, He's ready to forgive. *"I will heal their backsliding; I will love them freely"* (Hosea 14:4).

YOUR SPIRITUAL LEGACY

How will you be remembered? What kind of legacy are you building?

I pray that as you have read this book a new sensitivity to spiritual things has been activated in you. Your discernment has been awakened. You are a man or woman of purpose. You are equipped with a special gift from God to encourage and lift everybody to whom you are assigned. You will discern the hiss of the tempter, and you will recognize the still, small voice of God. Special promptings from the Holy Spirit will gently nudge you toward

> Jesus doesn't just want to be with you in church. He wants you to take Him home and into your daily life.

encounters with the right people in the right places at the right times, fulfilling the right plans for your life. I pray that your spiritual legacy will be worth remembering from generation to generation.

ABOUT THE AUTHOR

Jentezen Franklin is the pastor of Free Chapel, in Gainesville, Georgia, a congregation which has 10,000 in attendance each week. Named as one of the top thirty churches in America by *Outreach Magazine*, Free Chapel has recently grown into a new location in Orange County, California, where Pastor Franklin also speaks weekly.

Through his experience as a pastor, teacher, musician, and author, Pastor Franklin seeks to help people encounter God through inspired worship and relevant application of the Word of God in their daily lives. His nationally televised program, *Kingdom Connection,* is seen weekly on primetime television through various national and international networks.

Pastor Franklin is a popular speaker at numerous conferences across the country and around the world. He has also written several books, including the best-selling *Right People, Right Place, Right Plan* and the companion *Right People, Right Place, Right Plan Devotional,* both published by Whitaker House, and the *New York Times* best seller, *Fasting: Opening the door to a deeper more intimate, more powerful relationship with God.*

Pastor Franklin and his wife, Cherise, reside in Gainesville, Georgia, with their five wonderful children.